VISION MAKER

Three Weeks to Creating a Powerful
Directive That will Inspire Your Team
and Ignite Your Business

JIM BALLIDIS

Foreword by David Corbin

VisionMaker
Your vision made easy

Vision Maker™ is a trademark of Vision Makers LLC

Published by Vision Makers LLC

Printed in the United States of America

Produced by GMK Writing and Editing, Inc.
Managing Editor: Katie Benoit
Copyedited by Kelly Nutter Clody
Proofread by Lissette Lorenz
Text design and composition by Libby Kingsbury
Cover design by Libby Kingsbury
Printed by IngramSpark

Print ISBN: 979-8-9883417-8-9
Ebook EISN: 979-8-9883417-9-6

Visit the author at visionmakerbook.com

ADVANCE PRAISE FOR VISION MAKER:

"As a two-time Apple veteran—first during the groundbreaking launch of the Macintosh and later at the dawn of the iPhone era—I've learned and lived firsthand the transformative power of Vision. These weren't just products; they were revolutions, born from a crystal-clear Vision and executed to perfection. Yet, the alchemy of turning Vision into reality has long been an enigma. That is, until *Vision Maker*, by Jim Ballidis."

—**JB Herrera,** founder/CEO, Insight Driven Business

"*Vision Maker* ignites the flame of Vision, and collaboration fuels the fire that illuminates the path toward a better world for all. Love it."

—**Karen Gwartzman,** CEO, Retail Secret Circle and Private Label University

"You can create a Vision you love with *Vision Maker* because Vision is everything. A great Vision is worth millions…an ordinary Vision is worth a job."

—**Stewart Borie,** author, mentor, entrepreneur, and Wharton School of Business Strategic Advisor specializing in entrepreneurial management, capital acquisition, and environmental management

"I would recommend *Vision Maker* to anyone who wants to achieve their highest purpose."

—**Suzy Prudden,** CEO, Itty Bitty Books, bestselling author, and guest on Oprah

"So many dreams go unrealized because of Vision Killers. Jim Ballidis understands how to get visionaries to dream bigger and remove the obstacles in their way to unprecedented success. If you want to achieve transformational growth in your business or life, read this book and follow Jim's advice."

—**Nicole Schlinger,** CEO/President, Campaign HQ

"This book is everything you need to equip yourself with the necessary space for your big ideas to germinate and sprout—before the 'yeah buts,' 'what ifs,' and the 'how will I evers' take root and kill your dreams. A MUST to save a world of hurt for every big dreamer and entrepreneur!"

—**Lacey Haegen,** founder and CEO, Beaute Nouveau & Botanical Beauty

"'Motivating,' 'uplifting,' and 'inspirational' are the words we commonly referred to when addressing a book about personal development. This book certainly is all those things and more. Completing the book gave me the ability to recognize not only past successes and failures, but also a path forward that I hadn't previously recognized—a path to my Vision of being the best version of myself. I give kudos to the author, and I am very grateful for his work. I rarely read a book twice, but I suspect I will read this multiple times to stay on track with my Vision."

—**Paul Rhines,** CEO, Influence Mastery, renowned speaker, sales trainer, and author

"Jim Ballidis masterfully guides leaders to clarity and purpose in *Vision Maker.* Three weeks is all it takes to transform your team's trajectory and fuel your business with unparalleled passion. An essential read for those committed to not just leading—but leading with Vision."

—**Laura Leszczynski,** author of *Clubology: The Science and Strategy of Being in the People Business*

"Jim approaches Vision like no other coach I have ever had. Not only did he push me to make it bigger and then bigger still, but he convinced me it was possible. I am now aware of the Vision Killers, and I have also realized that my 'bigger than me Vision' requires a team to create it at the level it needs to be."

—**Adrienne Gordon,** CEO, Price Space, LLC, and Fortune 100 pricing expert

IF YOU DON'T HAVE A PLAN FOR YOUR LIFE, YOU'RE GOING TO
FIT INTO SOMEONE ELSE'S PLAN FOR THEIRS.

—Jim Rohn, American entrepreneur and motivational speaker

I would like to dedicate this book to those of us who have struggled to find a vision for our company and, in some cases, our lives. The evolution of vision creation will be nothing short of spectacular, and I look forward to each of us enjoying the benefits of a better future because of it.

Acknowledgments

I would like to acknowledge first and foremost my wife, Nanette, for without her extraordinary ability to create and empower a Vision, I would not be writing this book. Also thank you to Alex Mandossian, who empowered me to be vulnerable enough to tell my personal Vision Killer story, and to Gary M. Krebs, the editor who held me to my purpose and helped me with words, inspiration, and accountability.

I would also like to thank the following people for discussing my ideas, implementing strategies, or encouraging me to write this book: Allison Maslan, Louie Ortiz, David Corbin, Giles Fabris, Phil Black, Michael Bernoff, Paul Rhines, Nicole Schlinger, Cortland Warren, Mike Breeze, Mike Rees, Tammy Moore, Jerry Tracey, Tim Topman, Jacqueline Grant, Stephen Patrick, Kevin Crawford, Hawley Woods, Boby Gray, Lynn Rose, Paul Anderson, Dan Baily, Amr Bakr, Erica Balke, Ted Banzhaf, Bruce Bayless, Cameron Campbell, Stewart Borie, Lacey Haegen, Lee Clemens, Marshall Doyle, Laura Leszczynski, Corrine Rechter, Rachel Ramirez, Karen Gwartzman, Tim Camino, Shannon Brown, Brook Jay, Adriene Gordon, Dina Miller, George Lee, Pat Flynn, and a host of others who encouraged me all along.

And, if you are among the CEOs and entrepreneurs too numerous to name who said, "I want to get that book when it is released," please know that your affirmation of interest is appreciated and helped support this endeavor as well. As you all know, I did not want to write another book, but the subject is just too compelling to allow it to be overlooked any longer.

CONTENTS

Foreword

by David Corbin

Vision—what a powerful tool...or is it?

Many know me, and my penchant for candidly identifying the positive, AND the negative as we courageously illuminate our surroundings. Truth is that we can't solve *everything* we face...but we can't solve *anything* unless we face them. Illuminating and creating powerful visions has been useful for a small number of highly praised leaders, yet we need to face it...it's been quite elusive for many of us. Some honest souls will admit their vision just *sucks.* Good thing they do because those whom they are supposed to be leading have been thinking that for some time! There are quite a few books on the topic of vision—its need, use, and value—but none that I've found that lay it out quite as clearly, succinctly, and powerfully as the one you're holding in your hands.

We should be talking about a mental blueprint that guides our choices, shapes our journeys, and fundamentally changes the way we interact with the world. Our current lexicon of insight needs to expand further, to evolve, to become more adaptable. Happily, you'll find that his book delivers.

What I found in *Vision Maker* was an original, new thought, the start of a new chapter in that evolution, enhancing everyone's ability to create and reveal a compelling, useful vision for our personal and business journeys.

James Ballidis challenges us to recognize and overcome a powerful force that often lurks within. This is the force that clouds, distorts, or obscures our ability to create and reveal our unbridled vision. Ballidis refers to this as the "Vision Killer." Once identified and destroyed, we are unencumbered, empowered and free to create far more than we can currently see. We can now conjure what does not yet exist and step into the same shoes as those visionaries we admire.

Times are changing at breakneck speed. We must evolve beyond the successful methods employed previously. We live in a new age—an era quite unlike the industrial world from which our business ideologies originally sprouted. Gone are the days of the lone CEO, the experienced individual, who sees what needs to be done to solve organizational problems and single-handedly directs others to create a positive, profitable outcome. Sure, that model served and might well continue to serve us well when businesses are relatively simple operations. But in today's complex landscape, this old model falls perilously short.

To make the point, let me offer an allegory—a tale set in a vibrant metropolis, home to a seasoned architect named Elias. He wanted to create a marvel, a skyscraper that reached for the stars, a structure that melded classical aesthetics with cutting-edge sustainability features, all to grace the city skyline.

His vision was clear, and, as he had done so many times before, he began to execute. Each step was masterfully drawn, meticulously rendered. He added those features that would fulfill his vision. He presented the completed plans to his pleased client, who agreed they were fantastic. However, this also was true; the city, the contractors, the utilities, even the citizens were complacent and simply disinterested. In this context it's no surprise that the Vision Killers stepped in. As you could imagine, objections were voiced, by marginal but powerful interests, and sacrifices were required. Eventually the vision was rendered nothing more than a structural box of glass, mediocre and without heart. Elias was understandably distraught.

Now, let's reimagine the narrative in the following way. Envision Elias now as a maestro of synergy, a true Vision Maker and, thus, able to stave off the Vision Killer objections, build and share incredible vision, and obtain the support of those around him.

Vision Maker provides a three-week process for conceiving, creating, revealing, and actualizing such a vision. And now, with *that* in mind, picture the success *your* company can achieve when you orchestrate synergy within and around your compelling vision.

Fortunately, *Vision Maker* isn't solely a chronicle of the need to evolve: it provides an actual blueprint for changing our individual and collective psyche, and, dare I say, our culture itself. It embodies a purpose-driven approach, mirroring the essence of what I've been working with over many years of mentoring, coaching, and consulting. However, in truth, Jim just lays it out better and clearer than I could ever have imagined.

In a world of accelerating change, vision—of the right kind—is no longer a luxury...it's a necessity. Today's leaders must transition from being mere architects to becoming orchestrators of synergy, fostering a culture of collaboration, shedding light on the negative to cultivate the positive, and placing humanity at the heart of enterprise.

I wholeheartedly endorse this book as a vital resource for every leader who aspires not just to succeed but to achieve their true, extraordinary vision. I invite you to read attentively, internalize its wisdom, apply its principles, and I strongly suspect you'll experience how it revolutionizes not only your company but also the very core of your leadership and, yes, the lives of those whom your vision touches.

Let's embark on this journey together—a journey of vision, for the world needs synergy now more than ever. Let's be that Vision Maker.

—DAVID M. CORBIN, four-time *Wall Street Journal* best-selling author; two-time award-winning inventor; visionary, speaker, and mentor; founder, The Performance Technology Group; author of *Illuminate: Harnessing the Positive Power of Negative Thinking* and of *Preventing Brand Slaughter*; host of *Pass It On*

Your Vision Must Be Bigger Than You

VISION: *What we want to create in the future—*
that must come to pass.

Deep down, you recognize that you and your business should have a Vision—a powerful, impactful one, not just a throwaway phrase hung up in the lobby that nobody notices or cares about. Although you've managed to get to this point and achieve some measure of success with a Vision like *"To delight our clients"* (or with one that went by the wayside), you, your staff, and your customers are not inspired. After all, aren't you already expected to delight your clients and provide great service? You probably suspect that you and your company would be much further along if you had a *magnificent* Vision. You probably heard Apple's Think Different commercial, "The people who are crazy enough to think they can change the world are the ones who do." You realize you could make an even more spectacular contribution to your life and those around you with that all-important missing piece of the puzzle filled in.

You think to yourself…

Maybe we would see multi-million-dollar growth, instead of being stuck at six figures.

Maybe we would create some exciting innovative products or "customer journeys" to deliver services, instead of offering the same things over and over.

Maybe my team would feel more connected to each other and to the company's goals. Maybe my employees would love what they do, feel proud to work here, and be more excited coming to work every day.

Over the years, you've observed that the biggest and best organizations share at least three things in common: (1) they have a concise Vision statement that articulates what they want to achieve; (2) the words are bold; and (3) the messaging feels inspiring and timeless. Just a few prime examples from top companies come to mind:

- Unilever: *To make sustainable living commonplace.*
- CVS: *We will help people live longer, healthier, happier lives.*
- Disney: *To make people happy.*
- Google: *To organize the world's information and make it universally accessible and useful.*
- Harley Davidson: *To fulfill dreams through the experiences of motorcycling.*

Those Visions sound *amazing!* Who *wouldn't* want to work for these companies, do business with them, and pay for their products or services? While these statements are big-thinking, inspiring, and forward-looking, they are also credible and true to the brands and reputations of their organizations.

Do you long for your business to become more like these and create an exciting Vision? Suddenly, excuses flood your mind…

If only I had the time…
If only I knew how to get started…

If only I knew who to talk to…

If only I could come up with messaging that would excite people…

Guess what? In most cases, the excuses pile up and the leaders don't follow through on developing their Vision, despite multiple advisements from their trusted consultants, coaches, team leaders, human resource departments, and even the workers themselves.

Sometimes the company's leadership team heads off on a three-day, off-site retreat with the goal of creating a bright and shiny Vision statement. Upon their return, the heralded Vision is broadcast via email, posted in the lobby and/or breakrooms, and thrown up on the company website and intranet.

The result? *Crickets.* No one pays the slightest attention to it. It falls on blind eyes and deaf ears. As time passes, the Vision recedes into the woodwork like an old stain. The leader gets a whiff of what likely happened from random employee comments reported to him by team leaders and HR…

We had nothing to do with it…

Why weren't we involved?

It's a joke…

This doesn't mean anything to me…

It seems so out of touch…

I can't relate to it…

It doesn't feel like the company I work for—or even want to work for…

Ouch—all that time and expense wasted! I don't blame a leader for giving up after so much frustration and negativity.

Whether you've failed in previous attempts to create a Vision or have never tried, this book is for you. Discover why creating a Vision isn't just a "nice option," it's an *imperative* or there is an increased risk your company will fail in the coming years—or at least not realize its true potential. Remember the titans, Blockbuster and Kodak, that were too late to save their business because they lacked vision.

Vision is the future of business, and the future is here. It must be initiated with care, precision, thoughtfulness, creativity, an open mind, and a tremendous sense of urgency. In this book, you'll discover the tools and process you need to produce a Vision statement that will lead to exponential growth; company unity; and a passionate and dedicated work culture. You'll find yourself so revitalized by the statement that you'll notice you have an extra skip to your step each time you walk through your office doors. Every meeting with your team will be joyful, collaborative, and productive.

Best of all, you will accomplish this in only three weeks (also known as fifteen business days). What do you have to lose? Nothing! You've already paid for the solution, which you are holding in your hands.

My Vision of This Book

I began to create this book primarily for business owners, particularly those who are stuck at six or seven figures and can't seem to find a way to scale and transition their companies into becoming larger enterprises. They are often tired and frustrated from multiple failed attempts at scaling. They have been focused on executing their business strategies but ignore the fact that they are lacking a big, commanding, and exciting Vision.

Every concept and strategy I offer in this book has been tested on the battlefield with clients in my capacity as a mentor to CEOs, an entrepreneur, and an investor. I've worked with many CEOs who have been connected to a Vision that is bigger than they are and have then successfully grown and scaled their businesses, largely through the process I am about to share with you. At the same time, they have reclaimed their enthusiasm for their organizations and the thrill of the work they do every day. They live and breathe their Visions, as do the dedicated people on their payrolls.

The profound effect of this on business owners has enabled me to realize there may be even greater, more expansive benefits to be gleaned. A Vision can enhance our personal lives and those of our children and extended families. It can even play a significant role in our communities and American politics which, as we all must recognize—no matter which party we associate with—could benefit from a complete makeover.

I admit that this became a bit overwhelming to me when I first considered these implications. I wondered: *Am I stretching things a bit too far? Is my own Vision too big?*

I certainly didn't intend to write a lengthy Vision of my American life. So, I had to apply a couple of the techniques I advocate in this book.

There was one truth that kept consuming my thoughts. We all need meaning—in every aspect of our lives, not just business. While we don't want to "take work home with us" if we can avoid it, it's also impossible to completely compartmentalize our personal and business lives. We are essentially still the same people in both worlds, even though we wear many different hats and conform to the standards, behaviors, and protocols required of us in each setting. We occasionally think about business while we are at home (at least subconsciously) and about home while we are at work. Wouldn't it be remarkable if the same Vision applied in both worlds?

The Making of a Vision Maker

Are you wondering: What do I mean by Vision *Maker*?

Picture the *Makers* of olden times—clockmakers, winemakers, and toymakers, just to name a few examples—who ran shops with hand-used tools and instruments. They were regarded as magicians who brought things to life: clocks, wines, toys, and so much more. They were looked upon as craftspeople whose work went far beyond mere physical tasks. They sparked our imaginations, pushing the boundaries of our current beliefs and views. How might you produce a watch that requires no winding? When managing people to help produce their wares, a Maker had to hire the right people and train them, build and manage effective teams, and coordinate complex work projects to complete the final products, thereby fulfilling and perfecting the original Vision. In other words, the *Maker* develops an *army* of likeminded *Makers*.

For a Vision to stick, a collaborative team—just like the Makers in a workshop—is needed to develop the right messaging and believe in it with both heart and soul. Once the Vision is in place, the Makers have unified direction and are inspired to achieve greatness. The Vision Makers will spread the message far and wide enough to help it become a universally beloved (and profitable) brand.

Isn't this accomplishment worth a mere three weeks of your time and effort?

The Culprits: Vision Killers

If you feel stuck, lost, unfulfilled, or just plain frustrated in business and/or your personal life, there is likely a Vision missing that would otherwise be guiding your direction. Having answers to questions such as "Why am I here?" and "What should I do next?" are crucial to sustaining good mental, emotional, and, possibly, spiritual health, which impact every area of your life in some fashion. For many, unfortunately, that is not enough.

So, what stops us?

I see the Vision Maker journey as a great adventure with you as the hero. As in all great adventure stories, the protagonist must face off against formidable antagonists to achieve her or his desired quest. The drama wouldn't exist without at least one adversary throwing challenging obstacles in the hero's way.

Similarly, you would have little need for this book if you didn't already have opponents attempting to prevent the creation of a Vision. The twist here is that these foes don't necessarily have ill intentions. Sometimes your company CFO or COO gets in the way with excuses such as "We don't have time for that," "Squishy, touchy feeling stuff doesn't generate revenue," or "Why bother? No one will buy into it."

It can sometimes be just as dark at home. The moment you start to talk of your Vision, you are suddenly met with well-meaning but deflating recommendations. These folks may just be doubting Thomases or feel threatened by a Vision because they are change-resistant or skeptical by nature. They may also truly believe that the barriers they create are legitimate considerations "for your protection." In all these scenarios, the culprits may not even be aware of what they are guilty of doing.

How about an even bigger plot twist: suppose *you* are the opponent, whom I refer to as a *Vision Killer*? Like the adversaries on your leadership team (or anywhere in your organization), you are probably unaware of when you are the one harpooning your own Vision. Do not underestimate the power of these opponents—internal, external, or both. They may be crippling—or even shutting down—your business.

Allow me to confess how I happen to know so much about this subject: I used to be a relentless Vision Killer, working against myself and others. Years ago, if anyone—including myself—came up with messaging that contributed to a Vision, rest assured I was the one who was willing to take the other side and declare, "Let me play devil's advocate" or "It won't work." I would then proceed to explain all the logical reasons *why* it wouldn't work. I learned I had flattened the Vision of many great ideas long before they had time to inflate and take any kind of shape. After all, that is what an attorney of thirty-five years does, right? (No attorney jokes are necessary, but always appreciated.)

I've since seen the errors of my ways and want to help you identify and target your opponents. We'll navigate through those forces together, redirecting the Vision Killers in your path. You will feel a sense of achievement, comfort, and confidence as these individuals—including yourself, if that's the case—gradually enroll in your Vision as the creation unfolds before you. First and foremost, you must make sure the elements of a great Vision are in place.

Promises, Promises

There are several promises made in this book. They will not be from me to you, but rather, from *you to you.*

My Vision is not for you to become aware of your Vision and then just dabble in it. You need to become a true Vision Maker and be consumed by it. You must embrace it every day and breathe it in and out like oxygen. For these reasons, I ask that you make a pact with yourself to embed your final Vision in your DNA and keep it fresh and active every single day.

You will learn all the components to developing a great Vision from my program. If you are like me, you will often start a book, read it at your leisure, take a break, and then fail to go back and finish it. I totally get it, so I won't press you to emblazon every word of this book in your memory—or even demand that you read every single word (although that would be nice!). What I *do* impress upon you is that you home in on these four areas, as they will guarantee success as you create and implement your Vision:

1. Develop a Vision that is bigger than you.
2. Collaborate with others and feel the support for your Vision to grow.
3. Announce your Vision to the world.
4. Make sure you control the Vision Killers.

If you have all four of the above clear in your mind and understand the implications of each, you can rest assured that you will improve the lives around you and be well positioned to scale your business beyond six figures. If you would like to increase your likelihood of a successful outcome, please read on.

Three Weeks to the Perfect Vision

The "three weeks" time frame isn't hype or just a marketing hook. (Of course, *it is* a marketing hook in some fashion, but that's not the primary reason it's central to this book.) I've discovered from mentoring my clients that they are impatient people who crave immediate results. (Aren't we all like that to some degree?) They also want to see closure to the process—an end date. Most importantly, the system I propose *works* in those three weeks, at which point it becomes an integral part of your organization's natural ecosystem.

With the above in mind, I've organized this book in much the same manner as I develop strategies for my clients. It's divided into four even parts: the first three form the Vision Maker process; the final section concerns sustaining the beneficial results. I suggest breaking up reading into these weeks as well, so you will indeed have a complete Vision three-quarters of the way into this book.

Here is how each week breaks down:

- Week I, "What Is a Big Vision and How to Create It." I'll provide all the tools you need to get started on your Vision journey and potent weaponry to identify, battle, and defeat your Vision Killers.

- Week II, "You Must Successfully Collaborate with Others." You'll create the Vision Maker team, which will provide you with all the talent and forward-thinking ideas you need to get the Vision off the ground.

- Week III, "How to Evangelize the Vision to the World." This is all about the rollout and buy-in. If you can't overcome potential objections, you will never be able to get enough people to climb aboard and row the boat with you in unison.

- Beyond Week III, "How to Sustain the Momentum." This seals the deal. Here's where you learn how to ensure that the Vision—and, by extension, your company culture—is perceived as fun, positioned for growth, and—dare I say it—getting ready to change the world.

I've made every attempt possible to make this book as action-oriented, entertaining, and engaging as possible. Throughout the chapters, you will find in-the-trenches anecdotes (with names changed to protect the innocent) and special "Zapping the Vision Killer" boxes that serve as tips you can apply anytime.

Brené Brown, author of the bestsellers *Dare to Lead* and *Atlas of the Heart*, wrote: "We are born makers. We move what we're learning from our heads to our hearts through our hands."

What else is left to say, except: *turn the page, get out there, and make it happen*! Become that Vision Maker who finishes what you start and leads with Vision. It has always been in you, waiting to rise or rise again. Just listen to your heart and you'll know you are right.

WEEK I

What Is a Big Picture Vision and How to Create It

THE OLD MAN ON THE STUMP

An old man clutched his walking stick as he sat on a tree stump. He pointed the stick at Noah, a sixteen-year-old boy. "What will you be?" he demanded.

Noah proudly responded, "I see myself as a lawyer in front of a judge. I'm fighting for my client—whom I know is innocent—and making sure he is set free of a crime he did not commit."

The old man was amused by the teenager's answer. He lowered the stick and glared at him, as if looking into his spirit. After a solemn pause, he declared, "You are not the Maker of a big enough Vision."

Noah, greatly surprised, took a step back. "How could it not be 'big enough'? My parents told me I can't be a lawyer. They don't have any relationships with lawyers, which means I can't get a recommendation. They don't have any money to pay the expensive tuition. Not only that—my high school grades aren't good enough. So, that's about as big as I can see right now."

The old man stared at the young lawyer-to-be. Unintimidated, the boy folded his arms and stared right back. The contest abruptly ended when the old man asked, "My exact words were, 'What will you be?' Did I ask you what you could see—or what you could create? What you heard me say may lead to a profound discovery of your ability to make from nothing your desired future."

Chapter One

Controlling Vision Killers While You Create

n this chapter, you will be made aware of a formidable foe you will be facing every step of your journey to become a Vision Maker: *the Vision Killers.* I chose to address them in this first chapter because most business owners are unaware of their presence. They also don't realize that Vision killing has the potential to destroy creativity, energy, enthusiasm, forward-thinking, and buy-in long before an idea can germinate.

Vision killing may appear in several forms. It is illusive, sometimes shrouded and cloaked in good intentions. Business owners often don't realize the extent of the massacre until after the fact when all that's left of the initiative is a graveyard littered with whiteboard notes, old Post-Its, discarded memos, and lengthy reports that add up to nothing. They think about how much time was wasted in both tangible (such as meetings and research) and intangible (such as emotional energy and disappointment) ways that leave behind scars.

Anyone can act like a Vision Killer: a member of the senior leadership team (CEO, COO, CFO, HR director, etc.); department heads (sales, marketing, etc.); and all full-time and part-time employees (both on-site and virtual). Family members (such as spouses) and friends have also been known to blow-up a Vision in its early stages. In fact, as you will soon discover, *you* may be a Vision Killer and not even realize it.

Before we go there, however, it is important for us to first address the legendary Visionaries who set the standard for all of us to follow—especially in terms of their ability to defeat—or completely avoid—their own Vision Killers.

Acknowledge the Vision Makers Who Became Visionaries

Don't believe for a second that the world's greatest Visionaries were surrounded by "yes men and women" who bowed and genuflected when they heard their leaders' Visions. Many Visionaries—Albert Einstein, Thomas Edison, Mahatma Gandhi, Oprah Winfrey, The Beatles, Steve Jobs, Madonna, Bill Gates, Elon Musk, and those like them—faced significant rejection in the beginning and were subjected to more than their share of Vision Killers at one time or another.

What distinguished these legends from everyone else? What enabled them to rise above the millions of Vision Makers to become extraordinary Visionaries? They learned to hold their external Vision Killers at bay while managing their *internal* Vision Killers. In a recent article in Inc. magazine, journalist Jessica Stillman deconstructed an interview podcast between Lex Friedman and Elon Musk. In the interview, Musk admitted to profound fear when embarking on risky adventures. He relies on his passion for a cause bigger than himself and on a "fatalism" attitude about failure.

Musk and these other legends tamed their Vision Killers until they could create a Vision first, leaving execution for another day. Otherwise, imagine the daunting task of creating an Amazon, a Tesla, or an iPhone out of nothingness. We will add to this discussion by providing you with even more weapons to control the Vision Killer in you and others.

Let's consider another Visionary, Gene Roddenberry, creator of the original *Star Trek* series in the 1960s and its 1980s-90s successor *Star Trek: The Next Generation*. Roddenberry's Vision was to create a "*Wagon Train* (Western TV show) in space" and confront social issues happening at the time through the guise of science fiction. Though some people thought the show was silly at the time and several critics (including science fiction author Isaac Asimov) criticized the science, Roddenberry's Vision foretold incredible innovations that have since come to fruition: flip phones, tablet computers, desktop computers, hyposprays, Bluetooth, voice-response technology, teleconferencing, automatic doors, 3-D replication…you get the idea. An untold number of scientists, engineers, inventors, and astronauts entered their fields having been inspired by one of the *Star Trek* series when they were young. If Gene Roddenberry had listened to the Vision Killers and limited himself to only creating what was possible at the time of his shows, we would probably still be tethered to phone cords today.

The amazing technological innovations we currently enjoy are all the result of unbridled Vision. To begin your journey as a Vision Maker—and perhaps someday even become a Visionary like Gene Roddenberry—you must first learn how to lock, load, and fire at your Vision Killers and reprogram your mind. Welcome to Week I!

The Enemy within Me

As I mentioned a few pages earlier, *you* may unknowingly be a Vision Killer. Yes, you read that right. It's possible you've been killing your own Vision for years—or you've detonated the hopes and dreams of others without realizing you've been doing it.

"Who, *me?*" you ask. "I would *never* do such a thing!"

If you've ever heard the thoughts below circling in your head, you have Vision Killers lurking and waiting to attack…

I don't know how to create this thing.

I don't have the ability to see how it's done.

I'm not good enough.

No one is going to care about this Vision.

I've tried to create a Vision in the past and failed.

I've seen Vision statements in other companies and everyone either ignored or laughed at them.

I agree that it is unlikely you would ever *consciously* be a Vision Killer. But you might have been guilty of the crime, all the while thinking you were helping by sharing your brilliant analytical skills and years of knowledge. You didn't want to see a mistake made, so you splashed cold water on the Vision seedling, drowning it before it could take root.

"Come on, how do you know this?" you ask.

I know this to be true because, as I admitted in the Introduction, *I* was a notorious Vision Killer for years. No one's ideas were safe around me, including my own, if there wasn't an apparent reasonable method of executing the Vision. I'd say things such as "Nah, it'll never work" and then proceed to pile on heaps of evidence supporting my statement. All positive energy goes right out the window when an individual hears such contrarian language, especially if the Vision Killer is good at this job—which I was.

The book you are holding in your hands began several years ago as a simple realization that hit me after a three-day Pinnacle Global Network event (a world leader in helping companies scale, founded by CEO Allison Maslan) in San Diego, California. My intent was to glean some insights on how to run my business better. For many years, I owned and operated a successful law practice in California. Nanette, my wife, owned a separate business helping babies, teens, and adults relieve pain from various medical conditions utilizing natural, external remedy products branded Happi Tummi.

When she first informed me of the event, I had to control rolling my eyes. *Oh no*, I thought, *how boring*. At the time, I was far too involved with my practice and didn't subscribe to the notion that it was worth three days of my time to learn "one good thing."

We were also dedicated parents of three children and immersed in their activities: soccer, lacrosse, dance, cheerleading, and cross-country trips up and down the state. We subscribed to the idea that, if we didn't remain an influence on our kids, someone else would. While we enjoyed every minute, there were precious few times that my wife and I had just to ourselves.

That evening, I considered whether I'd had a knee-jerk reaction to being told about the event. I was certain that my wife had winked at me when she informed the kids that they were going to stay with their grandparents while we were at this three-day event. I interpreted her wink to mean that we would attend this event for a couple of hours each day and then, when the opportunity presented itself, walk a couple of blocks to the famous Coronado Hotel, sip cocktails, and sit on the beach, enjoying our alone time together.

Suffice it to say, this wasn't Nanette's plan. She spent all hours at the event enjoying her entrepreneurial adventure, learning, and networking. The part at the Coronado Hotel I regarded as "fun" didn't happen.

The trip wasn't a total loss. By the end of the conference, I'd obtained some excellent business ideas and strategies, which I implemented over the next six months. Whereas Nanette went "all in" and joined, I did not.

Six months later, she announced, "I want to go to the event again."

Oh no, not again!

Apparently, they organized such events every six months.

I admitted that my wife and I had made good progress using some of the techniques from the previous event. However, I didn't see any point to attending another one. It occurred to me that heading off to Coronado Island once again had an upside.

Golf!

I knew there were some prestigious golf courses in the area. I figured I'd put in the minimum amount of time each day at the event and then slip out to join some buddies and play eighteen holes while gazing at the beautiful scenery (since my scorecard would certainly not be inspiring).

As my wife and I entered the event, I rubbed my hands together in gleeful expectation of my escape to the course. I only had to put up with a couple of hours of this and then I could dart out.

To my chagrin, my wife insisted that we sit at the front table.

Damn. How am I going to exit without being noticed?

I hatched another plan. I decided that I would sneak out during one of the scheduled breaks; no one (except Nanette, of course) would be the wiser.

The morning session went well, beginning with Allison Maslan's introductory remarks. I found her to be charismatic and inspiring, as usual. She next shifted into what is refered to as creation of the Strategic Vision. Midway through her challenge for us to think bigger about our businesses, she called upon people from the audience to stand at a microphone and share their *Aha!* moments.

"What is coming up for you?" she asked in her inimitable manner.

Individuals proceeded to share their moving stories that led to their having experienced breakthroughs. Nanette unexpectedly stood up. I couldn't have been more shocked.

First, she insists we sit in the front of the room—and now she's going to the bathroom. She's going to march out while others are up there spilling their guts and allowing themselves to be vulnerable in public? How rude!

Something curious happened as Nanette headed to the rear of the room. Instead of going through the doors, she veered sharply toward the microphone.

I couldn't believe what I was seeing. Nanette disliked public speaking, and rarely addressed crowds about herself because it made her nervous. She didn't consider herself a good communicator on a stage, although she was quite dynamic with people one-on-one. And yet, there she was, up there with microphone in hand and addressing a hushed crowd.

She welled up in happy tears as she disclosed, "For the first time in my life I feel supported in my Vision."

My stomach became queasy. It dawned on me that, despite being her loving spouse and best friend, I was not supporting her in a way that made her feel her Vision was possible: a Vision to help millions of babies. I was a bloodthirsty Vision Killer. I felt mortified. I'd been inadvertently squashing her creative ideas and blocking her from carrying out her remarkable Vision by expressing why certain novel ways to accomplish her goals weren't worthy of effort. On further reflection, I realized that those comments were not useful or welcome during those moments of creativity. I felt embarrassed and ashamed of myself for having been so destructive, even though that hadn't been my intention. I should have been listening to the opportunity in her Vision, instead of reciting the challenges to executing her Vision.

Nanette's story was followed by a roar of hooting and clapping. As she made her way back to the table, mastermind members embraced and congratulated her on her success. I was deeply impressed by how much she had emotionally connected with fellow entrepreneurs.

I saw her in a new light—as a true Vision Maker—when she rejoined me at the table. Her Vision was not a goal or a target to achieve, but a Vision to impact the world. I became determined to honor her and avoid making this about me. I grabbed her hand, squeezed it, and smiled. She acknowledged my gesture with tearful pride.

At that moment, I vowed that I would no longer be a Vision Killer to Nanette. I would ignore habits that may have been useful in my thirty-five years as a lawyer but were a hindrance to others seeking to build their Visions.

Allison resumed the agenda, directing attendees to complete writing out a Big Picture Vision. The nine people at my table—along with everyone in the room—had their heads down, feverishly scribbling thoughts.

I froze, drawing a total blank. I couldn't come up with a single thing except: "To provide outstanding service to my clients."

From the stage, Allison shot a knowing look at me as if to indicate she knew what I was going through. She said nothing, however, and gave me a reassuring nod before tuning her attention to others in the room.

I became even more uncomfortable than before. In that moment, I had to face the realization that not only had I been a Vision Killer to others, but I'd also been one to myself. I hadn't dared listen to my own wants, desires, or abilities. Prior to that day, I only had a combination of frivolous, mindless thoughts and dreams of no consequence. I'd never given myself a chance to look inward and think about what I *could achieve* if I were to remove my self-imposed limitations.

I joined that morning and haven't looked back since. I sought to expand my journey and reverse my Vision-killing ways. Over time, I became so obsessed with the idea of allowing Vision creation while suspending the Vision Killer that I became something of an authority on the subject—primarily because I had the perspective of being a reformed Vision Killer.

Mark my words: You do not ever want to be a serial Vision Killer, as I was. The creative process must be nurtured, encouraged, and fed; it needs to be fueled by passion and excitement, so the best innovative and daring ideas have a chance to rise to the top and breathe new life into a business. When the Vision is done right, everyone in the organization becomes buzzed and energized, and outsiders clamor to join the team. Growth, expansion, increased revenue, and astronomical profits are just down the path blazed by the Vision—if no one guns it down first.

Who Was the Real Vision Killer—Noah or the Old Man?

How often do we limit ourselves regarding what we see, think, and know, missing the observations and recommendations of others? Did you accurately interpret the words of the old man in the story that begins this section? Did you accept that he was asking Noah about what he *could create*—or what the boy could see for himself?

At first, these may seem like trick questions because it is easy to erroneously deduce that the old man is a Vision Killer. In the moment, he might seem to be judging the boy; or at least the boy feels that way, defiantly staring back at the old man. But it is Noah who develops a feeling of being judged and limits his own opportunities by confining his Vision to *what he can see*. If this is never addressed, the wisdom of the old man will sail right past him, and he will focus solely on his limitations. As a result, he will fail to strive to achieve a true Vision and reach his full potential.

Goal-Setting Is Not the Same as Vision-Setting

During your time reading this book, I want you to focus on whatever Vision killing you might be committing upon yourself. I will show you how to manage others later, but for now, I want to make sure you start off on the correct path by being right with yourself. You need to make sure you don't push the "delete" button before you even get started. There will be plenty of time to assess *how* you will accomplish your Vision, but creation of the statement itself is too important to postpone.

Our self-imposed limitations are not unique or a personal "fault," but ingrained inside us. Over the years since your childhood, perhaps you were told (as I was on numerous occasions): *Don't get ahead of yourself.*

The notion of establishing "achievable, realistic goals" is planted in us when we are young and then drilled further the instant that we enter the workforce. We are told to "set attainable goals and then put together a plan to achieve them." This isn't a bad concept for accomplishing certain things, such as a college student who wants a good grade in chemistry class and puts into motion a rigid study schedule that includes supplementing it with weekly tutoring. The goal backed by a strong action plan results in the student earning an A in the class—*great!* However, that isn't remotely close to relentlessly creating and pursuing a Vision.

My point is not to say that goals are "bad"; in fact, they are quite useful and productive in many instances. Unfortunately, we tend to overly develop our achievement muscles and underutilize those that have the power to build a compelling Vision. Goals are practical and can guide you from step A to B. Vision takes you from step A to Z— and, sometimes, to a different alphabet entirely. The hyper-focused nature of goals makes it a Vision Killer because it forces you into a mousetrap of mundane tasks. Vision breaks the cycle and empowers you to believe that accomplishing the impossible is well within your grasp. Let's tackle some strategies to tame the Vision Killer in you.

Think Like a Child

Remember back to when you were young. Did you aspire to become a superhero? A major league baseball player? An astronaut? A celebrated dancer? A concert pianist? President of the United States?

Children have limitless dreams and Vision. To their young minds, imaginative play is real in the moment. They feel they can accomplish anything and have no reason to doubt themselves. From crawling to walking to potty training to talking, children are unconditionally rewarded and praised for each milestone. Every picture they draw is a masterpiece hung on the refrigerator. Parents, grandparents, aunts, uncles, and other family members and close friends hail them as prodigies.

Recently, I asked a fantastic golfer when he knew he was going to be "great" at the game. He responded, "I would play with my dad and his friends when I was young, and I would just go out and hit the ball straight. Their praise kept motivating me to be great." Soon enough, it became true; he started doing great things on the course with less effort. We want to be childlike when we pursue the creation of our Visions.

The Shift to the Vision Killer within Us

At some point during grade school, the well-meaning Vision Killers strike hard: Teachers, sports coaches, friends, relatives, and even total strangers start judging, rating, and comparing. The dream of being a major league baseball player ends as soon as a child makes an error that costs a game. The coach may attempt to make the player feel better, but the disappointed tone and body language say it all. Plus, the coach lectures the kid in front of the entire team—who may or may not be supportive. Deep down, those other kids are thinking: *Thank God it wasn't me! I'm going to make sure to never screw up like that!* Lesson learned, right?

The truth is, we all screw up at some point in our lives. Major league players make errors, strike out, and pitch meat balls that go sailing over the fences. A young singer might get nervous at her first live performance and botch a few notes. And yet, many people who experience such early failure never forget it and give up on their hopes and dreams—long after everyone else has forgotten the error that cost the game.

With each passing year, children become robbed of their creativity because they are told that they "aren't good enough" and start to internalize the words as fact. A child who thinks she's a great writer gets a D on one creative writing assignment and stops writing. A young ballplayer who is forced to sit on the bench through every game doesn't even try out for the team the following season.

Sometimes kids can be discouraged by the people around them; more frequently, however, they take their shortcomings personally and create self-imposed limitations. It's easier to decide "I'm no good" and give up—and who can blame anyone? Why subject yourself to more failure and embarrassment?

As a result, we reduce our expectations and learn to play it safe. We stick to the things that are simple and of lesser risk. Our dreams are often subverted in favor of following in the footsteps of a parent or other advisor and picking a career that is within skill sets that we perceive as limited. Our true Visions shrink or fade into oblivion.

What is happening here? We establish self-imposed limitations that stifle and sabotage our ability to challenge ourselves, think big, and create bold Visions. Our conscious and unconscious minds have developed powerful programs that block our ability to think and act like the uninhibited child within us who at one time was ready to conquer the world.

Can you guess the name of these powerful programs? *Vision Killers*, of course. And we—all adults, that is—have them running in our minds 24/7.

The Rise of the Vision Defenders among Us

We can all benefit from being more childlike as we prepare to square off against our personal Vision Killers. Children today are more encouraged than ever before to dream, create, and think big. This somewhat recent trend originates less from parents than social media. Have you ever had the talk with your children about their refusal to study in school because they are going to make a million dollars a month playing videogames on YouTube? I have.

Millennials Have the Right Idea

Younger generations (Millennials and Gen Z) often reject the limitations of Baby Boomers and Gen X and believe that anything is possible for them. This poses an interesting challenge for leaders and human resource personnel seeking to attract and retain young talent. The old way of thinking was that employees entering the workforce must "pay their dues" and work their way up the ladder. Many Millennials and Gen Z are confident they can start and run a company during or right after college. With a straight face, one bright Millennial worker who only had six months of experience as a junior account manager said to one of my clients, "I want to be your CEO in one year."

Millennials are fantastic Visionaries. They see, hear, and read enough success stories to reinforce the notion that groundbreaking success is well within their grasp. This means companies are not only vying for their attention, but they are also competing against their startup companies.

Leaders who regard workers from younger generations as "inexperienced upstarts" do so at their own peril. While many long-running, traditional businesses are floundering, the Millennial- and Gen Z-led businesses are eating their lunches and building organizations seemingly overnight that used to take years to create. I'm not diminishing the value of experience; it is vital in many circumstances. The issue arises when those years of experience become programmatic Vision Killers. If something didn't work in the past, why would we think it might ever work in the future? If the ideas of Boomers and Gen X decision-makers were shot down by peers and senior team members when they were just starting out and learning, why wouldn't they do the same to today's junior staff members?

What do Millennials and Gen Z have that earlier generations don't? Let's rephrase that: What *don't* they have that the older generations do? The answer: *limiting beliefs and views on dreams and Vision.*

Millennials and Gen Z are thriving because they have childlike mindsets. I'm not suggesting childishness in the sense of immaturity, but rather, they aren't programmed to shoot down ideas. They tend to love collaboration and even encourage creative suggestions from other team members.

When Vision Becomes Myopic

That's not to say Millennials are perfect in every regard. The problem many of them face is that, while they may have excellent Maker mindsets, they do not have the necessary experience to minimize the consequences of an error. Millennials and their predecessors can learn from each other.

The story of Elizabeth Holmes—the infamous founder of Theranos—is a cautionary tale. At nineteen years of age, Holmes dropped out of Stanford University and raised $700 million in capital for her technology that, she claimed, could test a variety of illnesses from a simple pinprick of blood. Holmes had Vision to spare and sought to become "a female Steve Jobs." The valuation of Theranos shot up to $9 billion in just a few years.

The flies in the ointment? The technology never worked. Holmes didn't understand the science and had no clue how to run a business, driving Theranos without a clutch. She created a business shrouded in secrecy and lies and fired and/or physically threatened employees who questioned their dubious practices. (Eventually, Holmes was exposed and convicted on four counts of defrauding investors; she is now serving jail time on an eleven-year sentence.)

Of course, we are all going to make mistakes (though, hopefully, not nearly of the same irresponsible magnitude as Ms. Holmes). The point is that a true Maker recognizes and admits a mistake right away, knows how to minimize the consequences, and immediately shift gears, repairing the damage and saving—if not furthering—the Vision. That is the imperative at this moment in time.

Being Childlike Is Easier Said Than Done

Imagine telling a business professional from an earlier generation (such as mine) to "think like a child." What expression do you see on that person's face? A total blank? A scowl?

Recently, I suggested to an entrepreneur who has built a $4 million business, "Be child-like in finding your Vision."

She was perplexed.

I pressed on. "Don't think of this as a task that must be completed before we speak again. Have fun, like children do. Pick it up, put it down—laugh and delight in the process."

She became politely defiant, wanting to understand while also refusing to let her guard down.

I tried a different approach. "Suppose I asked you to play superhero with me. How would you save the world from destruction from an evil entity?"

She cracked a smile. She thought about her response for a moment before describing how she would crush the villain with her superpower: her smile and ability to move others to action.

While in this childlike state, her inhibitions dissipated. She was now able to think big about her business and begin to create her Vision.

Children are excited to dream fantastical things and experience everything the world has to offer. They don't know fear of failure—unless it ends up instilled in them from outside forces.

Some parents of creative-minded children don't understand their longing to spend so much time dreaming. The thinking is that their kids will become lazy, ignore responsibility, develop bad habits, and not be held accountable; they won't develop the fastidiousness necessary to find career success. They want their children to follow them as role models.

I argue that the opposite should be done. When your children are granted sufficient time to dream and create without being bogged down with "the how," they originate remarkable concepts and/or devise new and brilliant ways of doing things. Of course, there is also a time and place for teaching children how to focus and execute as well. But the two cannot be conflated. If a child isn't given enough freedom to imagine and play, she or he may end up creating limiting programs that can hinder the ability to create an exciting Vision later in life.

As a business leader, you must make time to experience child-like fun and drop your façade when it comes to Vision creation. No one will judge you. Hopefully, by now you've figured out that you shouldn't judge yourself.

So, here is your challenge: During this entire first week while reprogramming your mindset to battle your Vision Killers, *be child-like*. Doesn't this sound like fun? I am giving you permission to play!

Reprogram the Vision Killers Within

Are you aware of the programs that are constantly dictating, controlling, and hindering your Vision Maker thoughts?

Consider the millions of people who have been unhappy with some aspect of their physical appearances and opt for cosmetic surgery. One might think their self-images would improve after the procedures have been successfully completed. As it turns out, this is far from the case. Studies dating as far back as the 1960s—such as those of plastic surgeon Dr. Maxwell Maltz, documented in his bestselling book *Psycho-Cybernetics*—conclude that patients continue to suffer from poor body image even after the identified physical issues have been resolved. Apparently, in many cases, the perceived problems weren't physical at all.

The takeaway is that the unconscious mind cannot be reprogrammed by any type of physical procedure. This means that, to conquer any Vision Killer in you or others, we cannot rely on physical or conscious methods of denial, confrontation, or logic. A charged emotional experience—such as the epiphany I had when I witnessed my wife speaking at the event—is required to zap the mind into identifying the Vision Killers.

I liken this to the "learned lesson" of placing your hand on a hot stove and burning yourself for the first time. For the Vision Killers to appear to you in their true form, you need to experience the scalding burn they are inflicting upon you (or you to others).

To experience this feeling, think back to a time when your dream was crushed. Everyone has had such an experience, so don't feel shy about admitting to it. How did you feel? How was it relayed to you? Where were you? What were you wearing? What was your reaction? Get in touch with that emotion. Once you feel the pain or fear coming back to you, think about how you will never let a Vision Killer control your future. Instead, you will choose to execute or not execute—but the Vision will remain until you choose to move forward.

The First Four Steps

In his remarkable book *Average Sucks*, communications expert Michael Bernhoff provides tools and profound techniques to empower us to step away from our embedded programs. The author attacks the foundation of why we often settle for less and creates a pathway for us to implement change. While you may not wish to undergo NLP (Neuro-Linguistic Programming) training or attend one of Mr. Bernhoff's communication seminars (although I recommend that you do at least one or the other), you can adopt his single most important technique to reboot your Vision Killer programs: *choose to change.*

Mark my words: Reprogramming your mind and implementing change is as simple as flipping a switch. While your Vision-killing programs have been well trained, heavily armed, and laser-focused on targets for many years, you can choose to treat them differently. You need time, care, patience, and practice to identify these programs. Once you are aware that the programs exist, you must stop them from running and redirect them by making a choice.

Actions to Take

Below are the first four essential steps you can take during your first week of my Vision system:

1. *Listen Deeply.* When you first hear or conceive an idea, your immediate inclination might be to take the role of devil's advocate, doubting Thomas, negative Nelly, or Debbie downer and say, "Nah, it'll never work and here are three reasons why." Instead of going there, do the one thing few businesspeople are genuinely good at: *listening.* Don't say a word (or react at all) to the other person who volunteers the idea or think anything else if it's your own concept. Just pause and *listen deeply* without judgment to others or to yourself. When you remain silent, you learn more in that moment from what you hear or think than you ever imagined. Remember the cliché, "You don't know what you don't know"? I would rephrase it as follows: "You don't know what you don't know *until you listen.*" When you interrupt the flow too soon, you block any chance of all the facts and perspectives emerging in full bloom.

2. *Be Curious.* I credit Pinnacle's Director of Training and JW Tumbles (a children's gym) founder Melissa Woods for having encouraged me to "be curious" during a training seminar a few years ago. You learn so much in the moment when you are curious. How do you demonstrate this? By posing *simple questions*—without judgment or agenda—to others demonstrating that you are paying attention and care about what they have to say. In response, they become encouraged to share observations that may illuminate your journey. When you stop being judgmental and ask yourself, "I am curious, why do I feel that way?" you become more willing to examine deeper thoughts and feelings.

3. *Be Present.* We all love our mobile phones and being connected to our businesses and important people in our lives. This also causes distractions, which can lead to overlooking obvious things. The *current* moment is the only one that matters. By being fully present, we give ourselves

the opportunity to observe and notice beneficial things. Shutting off technology at the right times (such as during a seminar or at a brainstorming session) helps us tune in better, which improves our ability to Listen Deeply (#1) and Be Curious (#2). When we clear our minds and enable ourselves to be more present, we silence the internal conversations and debates about the past and future, simplify the issue we are currently exploring, and become more receptive to new ideas.

4. *Be Fearless.* I didn't give much thought to fearlessness until I happened to review my notes on several different events, books, seminars, and experiences I'd recorded over the past several years. In every circumstance, I found words along the lines of "be fearless." The fact is that exciting things rarely happen if you aren't bold and take a chance every now and then. Even "luck" requires some amount of action and risk; a lottery winner, for example, had to act and spend money on buying at least one lottery ticket. I would also like to embellish this principle by adding some flavor: *be a hero.* Heroes in real life—just as in films—face things fearlessly, even when the odds may seem to be against them. In his book *Thick Face, Black Heart*, author Chin-Ning Chu writes about how we must be confident in our image of ourselves, beyond the judgment of others. One must adopt a fearless attitude, like a warrior. In doing so, great achievement is possible.

To begin taming the Vision Killers within you, treat the above four steps as affirmations. Write them down in a journal or another location you review with frequency. Read and recite them to yourself daily. Be mindful of situations when you need to apply them, especially when listening to new ideas or airing your own. *Awareness* brings you all that much closer to becoming a Vision Maker.

Let's get started with an exercise that helps identify the Vision Killers within you. Write down the answers to the following questions. Keep these notes, as they will become important as you venture into Vision Maker Week II and Vision Maker Week III.

1. *If you've never had what you consider a great personal or professional Vision of the future, what stopped you?*
   If you have difficulty answering this question, here is a Vision to uncover your Vision Killer attributes: *I want you to feed every hungry person in the world for one year without any cost to them.* Write down your response to that Vision statement. Are you thinking it's *impossible, stupid,* or *a waste of time*? Write down what you are experiencing. These thoughts are limiting your ability to create a Vision even before getting started. As I will explain later in this book, these Vision Killers are robbing you of the ability to collaborate with others and make things happen.

2. *Have you ever had a powerful dream—an earth-shattering Vision—for your business or personal life, but stopped pursuing or even thinking about it?*
   Write down that murdered Vision and do a postmortem. Was it a lack of money or resources? Did it sound too hard to achieve? These are classic Vision Killers associated with execution. Defeatist self-talk related to "how you are going to get it done" hinders your ability to create a Vision. To fend off this type of Vision Killer, set it to the side and make a note that you'll come back to it later.

3. *Whom do you consider to be a great Vision Maker?* Write down the person's name. It could be someone famous or a person you know directly. What attributes do you think make that person a Vision Maker? How would that person deal with the example you listed in question one?

4. **How would a hero act if she or he was faced with a villain (the Vision Killer)?**

    Write down what the hero would do to stand up to the Vision Killer in you and control the outcome. Again, be child-like. You can even write it like a comic book story if you want. Consider using your superpower—the one only you know about.

5. **What promise can you make to yourself that you truly want to keep?**

    Write down the promise as follows and then fill in the blank: "I promise that I will be strong against my tendency to _____."

If you went through this exercise and came up empty, congratulations! You have no issues. Consider yourself highly adaptive, creative, and open-minded. You think like a child.

If not, pay close attention to the Zapping the Vision Killer boxes scattered throughout this book.

Recognize That We All Have Multiple Personalities

Don't worry, I'm not a psychiatrist, and I'm not going to diagnose you. The heading above is intentionally provocative to make a point.

In her superb book *The Dark Side of the Light Chasers*, author Debbie Ford points out that everyone has multiple entities or personalities within us. (For example: I have lawyer Jim; father Jim; and quirky, funny friend Jim.) She notes that these deep-seated personalities aren't necessarily bad; they mainly exist to protect us. The strongest of these personas originated in response to an injury or hurt, to prevent or defend us against a reoccurrence. That presence needs to exist to safeguard the victim when a dangerous circumstance arises, but sometimes she or he appears at the wrong times and takes over, sabotaging ideas that might seem like a threat. Unfortunately, the fledgling Vision ends up being an innocent bystander and gets clobbered by this personality.

Ms. Ford recommends creating a private, beautiful place. Once there, dress the aggressive personality in your mind the way you'd expect her or him to look. Name this persona, assign attributes, and direct actions. Is this personality angry, frustrated, or fearful all the time?

Invite this entity to your sanctuary and conduct a meeting. Calmly listen to her or his viewpoint. Consider and acknowledge these points and thank that part of you for the warning. In the end, however, remind this personality that she or he only has one vote. You want to be alerted when something is way off base, but otherwise, do not be over vigilant. Each of your personalities gets a vote but not the right to veto another persona.

If this personality refuses to comply, you have every right to "fire" her or him from your board of directors, just as you would any real-life board member who breaks the rules. If the whole board is stopping you, fire the entire board!

Imagine what you will accomplish once you have exposed your multiple personalities and the Vision Killers within. You will then be in a prime position to let your inner child loose on the world, silence the Vision Killer(s) in you, and begin to joyfully create a Vision that excites you!

Chapter Two

Building a Strong Vision That Serves as a Protective Shield

As we continue, you'll need a shield to protect your Vision—one that is crafted to withstand intense pressure. You are its primary protector.

I'm going to ask you to be ultra-vulnerable as you seek to discover and unveil your Vision. Are you courageous enough to put yourself in this position? You must dispel the notion that vulnerability, that feeling you are susceptible to attack, is a weakness. Entrepreneurs have a particularly difficult time with this concept, as they refuse to appear as anything less than all-powerful—even to themselves. You need to replace this feeling with the recognition that the process allows a discovery of your innermost desires about yourself and the world around you.

The more vulnerable you become, the more likely you will be to uncover your Vision and express it with clarity. Most people don't examine their personal lives with this much scrutiny, let alone their businesses. I assure you that the long-term rewards and benefits far outweigh the temporary discomfort you'll likely experience. My recommendation is that you embrace these uneasy feelings. Regard them as confirmation that you are discovering new and different viewpoints and building strength from fresh ideas. Imagine how uncomfortable it was for early explorers and cartographers to draw new maps of what was previously believed to be a flat earth. Discover your true Vision and dreams that *must* become a reality in your heart because they exemplify your values and true purpose.

All this may sound overly dramatic, but it's not an exaggeration. I've spoken to hundreds of CEOs who are stuck in their businesses because they lack a true Vision. Vulnerability is at the heart of being "stuck." Being in this state exposes us to doubt, encourages us to flee to safety in numbers, and potentially causes us to remain paralyzed—the food of Vision Killers.

Makers like you will learn how to forge a protective shield by developing a deep satisfying commitment to the purpose of your quest. In time, you will discover that it's okay to feel vulnerable, and you'll develop a comfort level with it.

Set your intention that you will persevere in creating a deeply satisfying Vision that must come true—no matter what. Put aside the question "When shall it come to pass?" and use the exercises in the book to further your Vision.

What Is Vision?

Are you lacking a satisfying Vision? Or perhaps you haven't had enough clarity on what it is to create one?

To me, a Vision may be defined as follows:

A verbal, visual, and/or other auditory expression of your dreams, aspirations, and values. A Vision represents the things you grew up believing in or that you want to see realized in the future.

A Vision may serve as a way of being. It should be bigger than you, meaning that it serves more than just you and your clients and naturally resonates with others. In a sense, it's what you are called upon to achieve in a perfect future world. You may flinch at the concept that you are being called upon *to do* something, but that uncomfortableness is normal and part of what I referred to a few paragraphs earlier.

Start by writing down your dreams, your aspirations, and your values—the things that are most important to you. Use this day to write freely: *What you would love to see the world adopt in the future? What do you place great value in seeing?* At this point, don't worry about your business. We will bring it around, but first, explore the question: *What do you want to see created or accomplished in the future?*

Your Vision shouldn't be directly tied to your business and/or for yourself. Your Vision is like a play; the story is not about you, even though you are the lead actor. It's about a message or ideal that is greater than you. When you and your customers tell the story of the Vision, every audience will root for you to succeed.

In the beginning of this section, the old man asked Noah: "What will you be?" We've been trained to regard this as a question of Vision, but determining what profession we want to enter is a *goal*. Vision often gets conflated with *purpose, mission,* and *goals*. These three concepts are equally as vital and intersect, but they are not the same things.

- **Purpose** provides your reason for being and answers the question: *Why do I (and/or my business) exist?* Your purpose ignites your passion (which we will get to later in this chapter) and provides fuel every day for continuing your Vision journey. (For more on this subject, I strongly recommend Simon Sinek's superb work, *Start with Why.*)

- **Mission** distinguishes a business in the marketplace, answering the questions: *What does the company do, what benefit(s) does it provide, and whom does it serve?* A company's mission becomes a step toward securing the Vision's outcome.

- **Goals** are the practical and applied actions one must take at the present time to fulfill the mission, answering the question: *What tasks must we accomplish to fulfill our mission and bring us closer to achieving our Vision?*

- **Vision** is all about the future and, as mentioned earlier, answers the question: *What do we want to create in the future—that* must *come to pass—because it is connected to values that are intrinsically valuable for many people?* A Vision is the rallying cry for everyone directly and indirectly involved in your business—executives, managers, the workforce, vendors, consumers, and the community at large—to love and support the cause and, of course, the organization and its offerings. Vision is the foundational element that drives purpose, mission, and goals; it's also the desired result when all four are flourishing and working harmoniously.

Vision—distinct from the other three—overcomes the environment and limitations around you, instead declaring a powerful message of what you and your fellow Makers truly value. You know you've established a great Vision when you are all-consumed by it, and it is far bigger than you or your customers. The outcome isn't just about you; it's about everyone who is (or will be) impacted by it.

Your First Assignment

For the balance of today, do not read or explore the entire chapter. I'll provide a hard stop for you when the time comes. We are still in the first week—making great progress—but patience will be rewarded. Simply stay with the simple task of writing down your dreams of a better world, values you would like to see implemented, and benefits that other people would agree must be achieved.

Do not be afraid to write such things as "world peace." No one is looking. If it is truly important to you, put it on the page in your preference of large or small writing. I know, you are probably thinking: "Really? *World peace*? Come on." That is just a Vision Killer at work; your vulnerability is rising to make you feel like you are acting stupid. Build your shield by evaluating *why* you wrote down those specific words. Why are they important to you? Once again: Be courageous!

After all, what is wrong with world peace? If you are thinking or saying something like, "That is not going to happen," you are looking at *execution*—not Vision—and you must protect your vulnerable self. Instead of ridiculing the concept, ask: *Why is world peace important to me?* Watch the magic conjure thoughts you have long suppressed.

If you are stuck and unsure of what to write, try to unblock yourself using a technique inspired by *The Artist's Way*, written by Julia Cameron and Mark Bryan. At the same time of day during the first week, take out a large pad of paper and write for fifteen minutes. Don't even think about what you are writing; the subject doesn't matter. You can write about anything that comes to mind—work, your personal life, or even something fictional. Don't pause to perfect the exact right words, sentences, or structure or to correct grammar or punctuation. Penmanship doesn't matter, either. Just write freely without removing the pen from the paper.

You will not look at these notes again, as this is a type of mind download. Forgive the metaphor, but think of your mind as a clogged pipe that needs to be flushed out. To fix the cloggage, you need to run a stream of water through the pipe. The same goes for your mind when it becomes overwhelmed with random thoughts, ideas, and trivial stuff. Write it all down, then watch the discharge gush away.

After this mind dump, return to today's exercise. See if you can write anything down. If not, do not push it; sometimes it takes three or so days. Simply write what comes to mind. Each day that you feel stuck, rely on this technique. Most importantly, do not fret, as stress causes more Vision limitation. It will flow shortly. Trust that deep work on Vision always pays off with results.

Please take as much time today to reflect on this broad definition of your values, your dreams, and your aspirations. They will be important to reference in the coming days, so *do not go any further today*. Exhaust yourself by writing everything you can think of and don't be afraid to come back to this challenge for the balance of the day.

At this juncture, *stop!* You've done enough work for one day. Let it simmer overnight, and then you can begin the next exercise tomorrow with a clear and fresh mind.

The *Why Do I Want That?* Exercise

We concluded yesterday that Vision is all about the future and, as mentioned earlier, answers the question: *What do we want to create in the future—that* must *come to pass—because it is connected to values that are intrinsically valuable for many people?*

Today, I would like you to craft an answer to the question: *Why am I doing this business?* As you do so, avoid responses such as, "It's for the money" or "It's just what I'm good at." While both may be true, you may be sacrificing great personal happiness working in a business that drains you of energy, time, and opportunity. I'm asking you to probe deeply into why you do what you do.

This begs the question: *How do you begin to discover your true Vision—something inspiring that will breathe life and energy into your future?* It all starts with *you.*

Don't worry, we will solicit the help of other Makers and collaborate soon enough. Before we get there, however, I would like you to try creating your own Vision from your original, organic thoughts. I have good reasons for proposing you work on things in this order. Often, I have found that we—as well-trained entrepreneurial Makers—look for the easiest, most expedient ways to accomplish most tasks. When it comes to Vision, however, we aren't seeking to hurry things along and check off an item on our To Do list, which invariably produces a less-than-stellar result. We also don't want to bring in other people too soon, as we risk ignoring our own needs, inviting in outside Vision Killers, or perhaps copying the intentions and actions of others instead of listening to our own internal voices. Collaboration has an important place in Vision creation, but not when we are taking our first steps.

With this in mind, I suggest you try what I refer to as the "Why Do I Want That?" exercise. All you need to do: Look at what you wrote yesterday: your innermost desires of what you wish to achieve in the future. *Think bold thoughts* as you review your words, and add more as they come to you. As Allison Maslan might say, make it "big, hairy, and audacious."

For each desire you jotted down, answer the question: *Why do I want that?* Don't rush to draft your answer. Write what resonates for you, your values, and your dreams. Don't be shy or listen to an internal Vision Killer for advice on whether the desire is "realistic," "attainable," or "how you will get it done." (If you do, your Vision Killer will obliterate it before you finish writing out your thoughts!)

Next: Underneath what you've written, answer the question: *Why?* In other words, *why is fulfilling this desire so important to you?*

At this stage, a mentor—or imagining yourself as one—may be beneficial. If you wrote, "I want to serve my client well," a mentor might then ask, "Why is that important to you?"

You respond, "If my client is served well, they will keep using my services and I can make money."

The mentor voice would then take a step back and press further: "Is that all you want in life? To make money? There are lots of ways to make money. Why is *this way* so important to you?"

The mentor voice continues to ask the questions until you realize you have arrived at a truth—a value far more meaningful than the original answer. Maybe you conclude that "providing service" is a deeply rooted need for you to fulfill—but *why?* Perhaps you have a memory of a specific time when you were provided exemplary service that stuck with you. How did it impact you? As you can see, we're peeling back an onion to reveal a value or calling that is often hidden in darkness.

The *Why Did You Start Your Business in the First Place?* Exercise

You're now ready for the next helpful exercise, which also poses a challenging question: *Why did you start your business in the first place?* Most entrepreneurs and business owners who seek to become Vision Makers tend to answer in one of the following ways...

I didn't want to answer to someone else...

Out of necessity...

I fell into it…

I inherited it…

I wanted to get rich…

Your mentor voice digs even deeper: "Why *this* company? What did you expect it to do for you? Why have you kept it going for so long? Do you even enjoy it?"

Your responses to these questions will get your mind working and help you look through pat answers and expand your realm of possibilities. Keep asking until you have exhausted answers to the question, *why*? Ultimately, you will find deeper meaning and your *raison d'être*.

Spend the balance of the day continuing to ask yourself *why*. I can't tell you how deep to go; only you know the answer to that. The one thing I can offer to you is that, once you've pinpointed the basic need, desire, or value you wish to advance, your shield will have been hammered into powerful armor that can defend against any internal or external Vision Killer that might come at you.

Getting Unstuck

If you are still struggling to pinpoint *why you do what you do* after the last exercise, my guess is that you continue to be stuck. This is normal and even expected. Like a novelist battling writer's block while staring at a computer screen, you may be drawing a blank. Getting stuck happens to all of us—even when it concerns something as important as the future of your business. My journey of discovery and vulnerability may serve as an example to help you get past your blockage.

As I've already mentioned, by the time I came around to creating my Vision, I had a comfortable legal practice. Like everyone else, I had experienced my share of challenges and successes; overall, however, I was content with the status quo. Or so it seemed. There was a price to pay. I was bored—so much so that I couldn't motivate myself enough to come into work daily. If there wasn't something interesting going on, I would delegate it. I hired others, not to help my business grow, but rather to take tasks off my plate to make my life easier. Unfortunately, that was not a good prescription for my soul. In my case, too much leisure time led to distraction and indifference. This period was especially hard on those who cared about me. I was detached from my loved ones and wasted an untold amount of precious time excluding them. Without any kind of Vision to guide me, I was uninspiring to work with and be around. In other words, I was stuck.

I'm sharing this story because I know there are many of you who can relate to it in some fashion. I see little difference between my sorry state and the opposite extreme of being a workaholic. In both cases, the culprit is guilty of self-absorption, neglecting others, and failing to create and follow a Vision. To unstick myself, I came to grips with and shielded myself from the Vision Killer within. My Vision is far bigger than the one I had at that time, and you are now part of it.

Zapping the Vision Killers

Be the hero of your own story. Admit your shortcomings and challenges and claim victory by being vulnerable in this minute. Write out where you have been over the last few years. In time, you will discover a Vision that inspires you and takes you to a whole new level of fulfillment.

When internal Vision Killers start calling out the questionable parts of what you want to create, ask your inner hero to keep them at bay and silence them while you reflect by yourself for a few days.

Return to the last exercise with an intention that you will overcome the Vision Killer deep inside of you. Most of the time, you'll find the Vision Killer to be so strong that you lack courage to sequester it until a later time or remove it entirely. This is your chance! Dismiss the Vision Killer, be vulnerable, and focus your mind on completing the exercises for this day.

Stop here. Continue to refine and hone your answers. Tomorrow we will start to clarify your Vision by tapping into what you truly care about.

Passion and Vision

As you review your notes from prior exercises, answer these questions: *Do you have anything more to add? Do you notice any patterns or common themes? Does it seem like something is missing?* There are often multiple Visions at play, but my experience is that most share common themes; these are your *passions*, which typically percolate to the top.

Discovering your passions—outside sexuality, of course—can help you form your Vision. The search for your passion and your Vision for the future are both implanted in your DNA. Think of this in terms of other life forms. Why do salmon attempt to return to the same river from where they originally spawned? What drives birds to build nests in trees? Why do octopuses collect shiny objects? These habits and rituals go far beyond mere need; they are embedded in the DNA of these creatures and guide them on their journeys.

For human beings, passion is much more than a continuation of our species or the accumulation of things, such as wealth or knowledge. Internal passion must be so strong that it can weather the most powerful storm and help us recover from any setback. Passion infuses excitement into your activities as a Maker, even when you are at a low point due to external circumstances that may or may not be within your control.

Sometimes passionate frustration can also propel a Vision. Thomas Edison was so driven to create an artificial device for generating light that he failed thousands of times before successfully creating the light bulb. What activity are you so passionate about that you are willing to continue after that many failures (which, hopefully, does not happen in your case)?

If you have been feeling frustrated or disconnected during or after the last two days, ask yourself: *What do I want to do in life?* This simple question can lead to the formation of a Vision because the *want* compels you to continue in your effort, no matter what might be in your way. If the passion is coded in your DNA and lurking somewhere behind your every thought, it will spark a relentless pursuit of achieving something grand and spectacular: your Vision. If you see the passion in what you have written so far, record it as clearly and concisely as you can.

If your passion is not yet clear to you, then let's examine your DNA under a microscope. Try this useful exercise: Write down ten things you are passionate about and what you want to see for your business or yourself in a "perfect world." Next, go through each of your previous days' writings, aspirations, and wants. Do any of the passions you wrote down coincide with an item on your list? If so, write that passion word next to the corresponding idea. It may be beneficial to rewrite your entire list in a spreadsheet-like format. Across the top, write the aspiration, why you want it to be carried out, other parties who might be interested, and what is the passion within you that you are fulfilling. Can you connect the dots and determine which of the ten calls to you the most? On this day, you are starting to see your Vision come to reality. Hopefully, it is beginning to feel strong and able to withstand scrutiny. Why? Because you have identified a powerful passion, which is a formidable shield. But we have one more step to accomplish today.

Think Bigger!

The above heading is much easier said than done for some people. In this section, you will learn how to amplify your Vision as you have recorded it so far. To help you get started, let's look at a client journey I had the pleasure of mentoring.

A painting contractor (let's call him Ben) lacked a Vision when he and I first met. "I give great service compared to many others in my industry," he told me. His declaration wasn't a Vision, but rather, an appropriate mission statement. (Remember back to when we made the distinctions among Vision, mission, purpose, and goals at the beginning of this chapter.)

Ben needed to dive deeper. While the mission served his values, it wasn't shielded by the strength of conviction; he had to feel as if his conclusion needed to come to pass, no matter what. Budget constraints, hiring difficulties, and economic influences left his mission statement inadequate and irrelevant. While it was a fine thing that he provided great service, this was not a Vision. Like all other painting contractors, he was operating within the paradigm of juggling labor expenses and profitability with seasonal and inexperienced help.

In the months that passed, he made numerous unsuccessful attempts to look within and find a path toward conveying his Vision. Suddenly, one day he called me in a frenzy of excitement. He'd managed to clear his mind and specify why he had created his business. His Vision went beyond his desire to be an entrepreneur and any financial benefits. He didn't even care about painting houses; this wasn't his passion. However, he *did* have a strong desire to create a better quality of life for himself and those who worked for him. He wanted to offer more substantial benefits and higher pay to painters who sought to make it a full-time career. This type of worker is notoriously scarce; many are available sporadically depending on the season and/or whether they have other supplemental jobs.

Ben created a new Vision that revolutionized the painting industry: "Every person has a right to a profitable and successful *career*, not just a job, that helps them provide for their family." Realizing that he was able to impact the painting industry, he conceived a painter's college designed to train professional painters for his workforce, as well as other employers in the area. Graduates would work faster and without mistakes which, in turn, would generate better quality work, make them more reliable and professional, and teach them indoor as well as outdoor painting to diversify their skills. The enrolling students wanted to make a career of painting but could not afford on-the-job training, seasonality, a demotion, or a layoff when work was slow and due to others' seniority.

The outcome would be nothing short of miraculous. The graduates would become more dedicated to their careers and far less likely to leave for another industry. They could be paid more because they performed the work faster, at a reliable pace, and with fewer errors, which meant the initial estimates would be far more accurate and the business infinitely more profitable. Interestingly, the bigger Vision fell prey to postponement (another Vision Killer), but word spread about the program and its obvious potential success, which gave rise to a smaller version. Ben no longer had to scramble to find painters to fill his clients' needs; a stable of skilled workers at the ready arose from this smaller form of Vision in the infancy of development.

Other unexpected rewards surfaced. The trainees felt a certain pride in their work and newfound knowledge. Many began to demonstrate a brand-new trait: *leadership*. Several wanted to become team leaders on painting assignments; others followed a path to become teachers.

Big Visions don't stop with the workforce, the company, the clients, and you. The painting college will be financially supported by large paint supply companies, who sponsor scholarships and donate money, time, and resources. This can lead to better relations between paint companies and their communities. By providing value to an underserved aspect of the painting industry, Ben built *careers* for people that ultimately meant greater opportunity, higher wages, and improved benefits. His company not only grew and gained profit, but even more importantly, it also earned a legacy of trust. By having developed a clear Vision, Ben created a much more fulfilling life for himself and his workforce, even though his Vision is far from being fully implemented. It is important to point out that great Visions make steps toward success during implementation, and along the way, results are achieved. Visions that are early victims of the Vision Killer simply never get a chance. That is why it so important to suspend your concerns at the early stage of Vision Making.

Do you detect the passion in this case study? Is there something in your writings that is like Ben's experience? Don't let your shield down to evaluate how you will get it done. Ben didn't choose an easy or hard path; he followed a passionate desire. You can, too, but at this point you must *think big* and hold your protective shield up high.

Another remarkable Vision was introduced to me at a recent event at my son's high school. Nick Jordan, CEO of the nonprofit

Wells for Life, proclaimed the following in a well-tailored Irish accent: "No child in the world should be without clean drinking water." The inspiring message and ultimate future achievement are both succinctly conveyed in these dozen words. His specific goal was to "Help a million people." Nanette and I were riveted and joined the cause. Who *wouldn't* want to ensure clean drinking water for children and help achieve that one million goal?

Nick is an inspiring person, undaunted by the massive size of his Vision. Later that day, he shared the news with Nanette and me: He had reached the one million people target. What an achievement!

Let's pull back for a moment. Imagine if Nick's Vision had been to "Drill wells for those in need of fresh clean water." Would you feel as inspired by this as his actual Vision statement? The word "drill" is unpleasant, but that's beside the point. The main problem is that it goes too far in terms of implementation. Who cares *how* the clean drinking water is obtained? Additionally, the language "those in need" sounds softer and less urgent than "no child in the world should be without." Nick's passion comes shining through his word choices, which compels others to want to jump on the bandwagon and ask, "How can I help?"

Review the Vision Maker Process

Let's do some accounting of what you've learned so far in this chapter:

- You understand what Vision is and how it is distinct from purpose, mission, and goals.
- You can answer *why* you do what you do, thanks to the "Why Do I Want to Do That?" exercise.
- You've zapped a Vision Killer (or two).
- You've discovered how to think like a child to free your mind.
- You've unstuck yourself from whatever is holding you back from expressing your Vision.
- You understand the correlation between passion and Vision.
- You've learned to *think bigger*.

Guess what—you are officially ready to start making your Vision!

Find a comfortable, peaceful spot that inspires you and where you won't be disturbed or constrained by time. Turn off your phone ringer and alerts. Clear your mind with a few deep breaths. As you begin, loosen up and have fun. Don't pressure yourself, overanalyze anything, or make the process complicated.

Read over your list of either organized or scribbled down gold nuggets from prior writing sessions. Select everything that stands out to you, even if the concepts aren't fleshed out. Now, start to write down a few ideas and thoughts based on your nuggets and/or anything new you come up with. The wording is unimportant; just let it all flow out. Don't rush or worry about perfection. You will be able to refine it later. In fact, as you write out each idea, leave space beneath it for revisions.

You may find yourself getting into a groove—fantastic. Keep going! Don't stop until you have nothing left to write.

If, however, you're feeling a little lost, don't despair. You're not alone. Be patient with yourself. Take a walk or listen to music, and then return to it.

If you continue to be stuck, think about things that arise from your work, your home, your marriage, your family, or your community. A starter Vision might be something as basic as "I want a peaceful marriage" or "I would like to be recognized for my contributions in my company."

At this early stage, it doesn't matter what you write or its quality. You are the Maker of your own future. Your Vision can be whatever you want it to be. There isn't a time frame for completion; no alarm goes off to signal you need to be done. Trust me: your Vision will continue to grow, evolve, and blossom. Before you get to Week II, however, you need to pull out your weapons arsenal and wage an all-out war against your Vision Killers. Keep them in check with the shield of your conviction that what you've created is authentic, real, and powerful—bigger than you and worthy of others' time and consideration.

We will now expand on that Vision in the next chapter, which occurs on day four.

Chapter Three

Taming Vision Killers with a Bigger Vision

So far, you've been spending most of the first week of the program as a Maker creating a Vision that is driven by passion and is intrinsic to your values. Thanks to your hard work, your budding Vision is starting to form a relationship with your business, in addition to its significance in your personal life.

In this chapter, you will discover how to make your Vision so strong that the Vision Killers won't stand a chance in their attempts to derail you. Instead, you'll learn how to win over and convert them into becoming powerful defenders of your Vision. Sound impossible? Just wait.

Think EVEN BIGGER

Your first step is to create a Vision that is at least *ten times bigger than you.*

Allow me to illustrate what I mean by this. If you were to propose a Vision along the lines of "I want to earn a million dollars," who else would bother to help you? Probably no one. Why? Because that is a goal, not a Vision—a distinction we clarified in the last chapter. Pursuing a specific, task-oriented goal instead of a future-thinking, expansive Vision is a common trap among unwary entrepreneurs.

Now, let's suppose we were to make a simple tweak to elevate that goal language: "*Feed* a million starving people." If you were to propose that as your Vision, and you showed an unwavering decision to build on it, how do you think your key stakeholders would react? After overcoming the initial "How will you do that?" Vision Killer questions, my hunch is that they would eagerly hop aboard this bandwagon and put in an extra 10% (on top of the current 100% effort) to help make it a reality. Who wouldn't want to feed starving people? Would anyone balk if you also happen to earn a million dollars in the process? Highly unlikely. They would probably pat you on the back and say you deserve every penny. The point is that Visions bigger than you are always supported and their benefits will naturally find their way to you. So, do not limit the size of your Visions.

> Big Visions inspire people to recruit others, which reduces the number of Vision Killers and weakens those that may linger. There is great power in numbers!

Big Visions Lure Supporters

More importantly, a Vision such as "Feed a million starving people" would be what I refer to as "Vision Killer–proof." Your emotions and intelligence would become so enamored with it and fueled by such passion that your internal Vision Killers would be too embarrassed to pose any kind of threat. External Vision Killers—who may be any-one in your proximity—would be supportive of this Vision because it's about something much bigger than just you: *helping other people*. They will also be more inclined to take the initiative and become an influencer, spreading the messaging about your Vision and increasing the number of cheerleaders banging the drum for it. But I know what you may be thinking: "There are lots of entities that have this Vision, some more successful than others—so Vision may not be the answer." Please suspend that Vision-killing messaging until later in the book. As you will see, there are other crucial steps that haven't been utilized by every entity or person wanting to accomplish such a Vision. The development of a complete Vision is needed, which includes more succinct efforts outlined in later chapters.

I hope you are beginning to follow an assertion of mine: *A Vision larger than you is never wrong.* You may encounter several challenges and obstacles while achieving it, but it is only faulty when the Vision *isn't* big enough. No one would ever dare assert that a Vision bigger than you is unworthy of discussion.

One simple test to determine whether your Vision is substantial enough is to ask yourself the question: *Does anyone else care about it?* If the answer is *No*, then you have more work to do. You need to create something even more expansive that will ignite passion among others. If you think along the lines of how your Vision can improve our world and/or answer a universal need or want, you will be on the right track.

Social Justice Messaging Is Wonderful but Not Obligatory

It should also be stated that touting a social cause is not a requisite for a strong Vision. It's great if that happens to be the case, but by the same token, you shouldn't force it, or it risks being unauthentic. The cause needs to fit in with your future desired state, reflect the benefits of your business in some way, and make coherent sense alongside your company's brand.

You may be grappling with what Vision you can create that is larger than you but doesn't involve social justice. There are plenty of businesses that simply provide a desired service or product that solves a problem or fills a desired need without being "do-gooders." There is nothing wrong with this. I'm not here to judge. However, even organizations such as these must still have *bigger* Visions that many people care about.

There are myriad approaches to this, so the best way to get your creative juices flowing is through an example. Stephan, a client of mine, owns several profitable medical spas. Despite his success, something was nagging at him, and he simply couldn't put a finger on what it was.

Stephan is a brilliant businessman. His medical spa provides services that improve the appearance of unsightly scars, blemishes, discolorations, skin defects, and tattoo removals. When he discusses the business, he describes it in terms of productivity, fair pay for his workers, and a high level of service for his customers. His management style is a perfect example of proper goalsetting and execution.

During my sessions with Stephan, he disclosed that his Vision was something along the lines of "the delivery of great service to those that would seek to change their appearance for the better." He was passionate about offering safe and effective medical procedures, especially because competitors often fell short in this regard, and he would hear the complaints. Sometimes his medical facilities ended up correcting the mishaps of others.

While Stephan's business practices were (and continue to be) exceptional, they weren't big enough to serve as a Vision. I encouraged him to dig deeper, as I prodded you to do in the last chapter. After some back-and-forth, he shared his belief that his spa's services enhanced his customers' self-image. As it turned out, he had a great deal of pride and passion for this result—even though he hardly ever discussed it.

Aha! Enhancing customers' self-image is a *massive* promise and more than grand enough to serve as a Vision, especially since Stephan had the power of passion driving it. Is this value a social cause? No. It's still a great Vision, however, as it can improve the lives of many people—and there is even more here to uncover.

Now that we had pinpointed his Vision—something that existed all along in his mind—I asked why he hadn't shared his passion more often. He responded, "Few people would care, other than those who obtain the services." In other words, he was saying that promotion of his business was limited primarily to those who happened to be seeking services.

I thought for a moment before following up with another question. "Do you think it's possible for me to refer someone to you who has low self-esteem due to an issue with her appearance?"

"Sure, I hope so," he answered.

A lightbulb went off as he realized what he had just said. Right in front of my eyes, Stephan began to radiate energy. He instantaneously became reinvigorated in his business. Rather than simply offer his company's services, he became emboldened to place the Vision at its center and share it as far and wide as possible—with customers and noncustomers alike.

Stephan's nagging feeling disappeared. He made plans to expand his outreach—first to three new locations and then to one hundred—based on his Vision to help people improve how they felt about themselves and their appearances. His relationship with his customers no longer felt transactional, as he was helping them resolve a much more substantial issue on an emotional level, in addition to the physical benefits offered. He realized that his customers (past, present, and future), workers, stakeholders, and vendors would all be proud to be part of this effort and help him spread the word of these wonderful benefits. Helping people feel good about themselves may not resolve a social injustice, but it is absolutely a universal desire sought by a significant number of people.

Seven Ways to Make Your Vision More Powerful

Some types of business ventures aren't as easy as others when it comes to pinpointing and expressing a Vision that will inspire others. For example, a company that manufactures widgets would probably struggle with this more than a medical spa. A company that handles tree removal might also struggle at first—until the CEO realizes that her company improves sustainability and beautifies neighborhoods, benefits that appeal to a lot of people who don't even claim to be "tree huggers."

Obviously, I don't know what your enterprise does for people or how it may be distinguished from its competitors. However, I can provide seven concrete steps to help you formulate a bigger Vision that will inspire others and ward off any internal or external Vision Killers.

1. *Determine what your profession does for society.*
   I met with a software coder, Zack, who struggled to figure out the above. When I asked what he did for a living,

he had difficulty discussing it. How can a software coder make his career more interesting and appealing on an emotional level? Don't most people perceive it as technical and boring?

Everyone can relate her or his work to society in some way. When I challenged Zack in the same way as Stephan, he explained that he wrote code to protect people from online identity theft when they are doing online transactions. He helps online customers shop safely and feel comfortable while doing it. This is a much needed and appreciated service for society! All Zack needed was to make a small adjustment to his daily objective and he had identified a powerful Vision for himself.

2. *Connect a personal passion with your business.*
One evening at a cocktail party, I engaged in a conversation with Oriella and Ned, a couple from New Orleans. When I asked Oriella what she did for a living, she replied, "I make gift packages for people." I detected a lack of enthusiasm for a business she had been running for a decade and a half.

I know what you are probably thinking: *Oh boy, here comes Jim again with his pitch for originating a big Vision!* If you predicted that I was going to meddle in guiding Oriella toward a bigger Vision, you would be 100% correct. I couldn't help myself because spreading the benefits of Vision creation is part of *my own* Vision!

"Okay," I said. "You've identified what you *do*—but what is your *Vision*?"

"Um," Oriella pondered, thinking I'd asked a trick question. "I please my customers."

"Excellent," I said. "But, you know, that's not a Vision. You need to state *something bigger* that you are truly passionate about. I'm not feeling your passion—although I'm sure you have it."

I'd given Oriella some food for thought. A few days later, I happened to meet up with the couple again during a speaking event. I barely had a minute to spare, but I spent time with her because I could tell she was anxious to share something important. Oriella spoke with such breathless ebullience, she seemed like an entirely different, animated person. "I have it, I have it! I know my Vision!"

"What is it?" I asked with great interest.

"I enjoy enriching the art of giving to those who are challenged to think of unique gift ideas," she answered.

"That's wonderful!" I exclaimed.

She went on to inform me that the new Vision already inspired her to implement several new market messaging strategies and create new products. Most importantly, the Vision instilled newfound energy and purpose, which was especially critical because Ned—who owns and operates a business of his own—had been a Vision Killer for hers, having concluded that the business hadn't been worth his wife's aggravation. Once he heard Oriella's new Vision, however, he did a complete reversal and became her number one supporter. Her passion for her business had rubbed off on him. When I saw Oriella four months later, she ran up to me and gave me a warm hug.

"My favorite New Orleans couple," I said. "How are things coming along with your gifting business?"

She couldn't wait to provide an update. Not only was she achieving more financial success, but she was also able to revel in witnessing the excitement among her staff when they speak to customers and each other. This same thing can happen to you once you connect your passion to your business.

At her events, Allison Maslan asks people in the audience to create their strategic Visions. Afterward, she tells them to *triple it*. Every time she does this, gasps of fright ripple throughout the audience. There is a cogent method to her approach; she is forcing everyone to set aside their Vision Killers and allow room for big thoughts and passion to emerge.

3. *Think of ways in which others will love you for what you do.*

This is a tough one for many people. They are battling a fierce inner demon who says, "You are not worthy of love."

I don't care what any voice in your head tells you. You *are* worthy! Here's what you need to do: Consider what your customers love about what you and your business provide for them.

Monica, a wonderful woman and brilliant marketing consultant, struggled to find her Vision. When I asked her to focus on what her customers love about her and the service she provides, she became embroiled in emotional turmoil. She confided in me that she had been raised in an unhealthy environment and later had endured abusive relationships. She hadn't even considered that her clients might love her. The more she thought about it, the more she realized they deeply loved everything she did for them.

I believe it's almost always possible to find a way to derive some benefit from the past—even one that includes unpleasant experiences. In Monica's case, she developed a unique passion for doing the right thing and personally taking responsibility for the outcomes she created. "I treat them like they are my babies," she reflected, in reference to her marketing campaigns. Public and private companies of all sizes wanted the special care and attention only she could provide to them. Once she arrived at this epiphany, her opportunities exploded because she was able become a Maker and create a Vision that communicated this messaging.

4. *Look at the business through someone else's eyes.*

Sometimes we get tunnel vision and cannot see our business

as objectively as people looking at it from the outside. My wife will constantly point out things that she admires in me that I don't see myself. Upon reflection, I realize this is because I'm too close to the picture.

A coach can often be of help overcoming this limitation, but you are also capable of doing it yourself. All you need to do is imagine yourself standing in your customers' shoes. From this perspective, why do you think they choose to work with you over a competitor? If you have tangible evidence to support this—such as a verbal or written thank you in which a customer complimented you and/or your business—accept the words as fact!

5. *Continuously repeat to yourself why you created and continue to operate your business.*

Recently, I had the pleasure of chatting with an extraordinary entrepreneur, Tim Topman, who created an online training experience in which music teachers train other teachers. His initial Vision was to modernize music teaching for a new type of student and provide educators with the ability to profitably teach in today's environment. He is passionate about his business and has created several courses and a podcast that have garnered worldwide influence. I met with him to chat about my unused grand piano; the conversation eventually shifted to his desire to expand his message to others. He spoke about his frustration with the mindset of teachers, who rely on old teaching methods that are dependent on public school funding. Meanwhile, today's students have shorter attention spans that don't work with traditional methods.

I asked Tim why these things were important to him, and he expressed his concern that budget cuts and governmental reductions in school programs in the United States and Australia are causing serious harm to musical education and appreciation. Fewer children and young adults are being exposed to learning to play musical instruments, the pleasure of hearing different types of music, and the richness of music history and theory. It has been scientifically proven that music has a favorable impact on strengthening and broadening young minds; without it, their brains will be deprived of something essential to their development.

Tim and I soon realized we shared a bigger Vision. Music is profoundly important to both of us, and we agreed that something must be done to rectify this growing problem.

His new Vision does justice to the cause and can most certainly be considered "big enough":

Music should be kept in schools because it is so vital, so valuable, even if schools or state budgets will not pay for it.

In this instance, the Vision Killers are truly formidable. They might include anything from "How are you going to possibly accomplish that?" to "Where is the funding going to come from, if not the government?"

Perhaps you've already figured out why these two foes are inappropriate in the context of Vision. If you stated they are both about execution, you would be 100% correct. So, recognizing this fact, how does Tim ward them off? He must repeat the following with conviction ad nauseum: "That sounds like good observations in execution, but let's just talk about the Vision for a moment. Shouldn't music stay in schools, even if the government cannot or will not fund it?"

If you are concerned that your Vision is just an exercise in futility, hold your course and continue! Continuously remind yourself why you created and operate your business in the first place. This makes striving toward achieving your Vision too important to even consider throwing in the towel.

As of this writing, Tim doesn't yet know how he will accomplish his Vision. It's only been a few days since we discussed it, and we know Rome wasn't built in a day. I'm also confident that Tim is more than up to the challenge because his Vision is so strong, and he passionately revisits his *why* on a regular basis.

6. *Expand your Vision if it addresses a need or a fear.*
Often a Vision is designed to help individuals overcome their fears and feel secure. Consider, for example, the American/Soviet Union Cold War, when the United States amassed a multi-billion-dollar war machine over the course of several decades. The Vision for America was one of safety, to protect the American way of life—especially against the possibility of a nuclear attack. The effort worked and sustained itself, whether the threat was imminent or not.

In the case of your Vision, consider whether your business is addressing something that may cause harm to many people. MADD (Mothers Against Drunk Driving) set out to curb drunk driving casualties. The threat of teenage sons and daughters being maimed or killed in a preventable accident appealed to mothers on such an emotional level that they felt compelled to take immediate action and carry forward the Vision.

If your Vision promises to alleviate a fear shared among many people, the response will be an outpouring of support to amplify the outcome and make it bigger. In this way, you can solve more than just your circumstance and help make a better world.

7. *Expand a Vision that innovates and makes things faster, more reliable, more enjoyable, or just easier.*
Steve Jobs, the cofounder of Apple, envisioned "a computer for the rest of us." Talk about innovation at the highest level! Prior to Mr. Jobs, computers were regarded as machines that could only be used by techies. Thanks to his inspired Vision, the entire computer industry had

to up its game and create products that appealed to every consumer—not just computer experts, but everyone from little kids to grandparents. People were thrilled and proud to embrace Apple's myriad innovations, as all of them contributed to an improved experience with technology that made their lives better.

How a Visionary Tamed a Vision Killer

So, what does a Vision bigger than you look like? Martin Luther King Jr. said it best: "I have a dream."

Dr. King was a charismatic and brilliant speaker, but it wasn't merely his vocal talent that carried his speech into greatness; it was his willingness to have a dream ten times bigger than himself. If you listen to his speech, you will hear his inclusion of all races, genders, and nationalities; it is a Vision of equality for everyone, not just one group. While his Vision has been shared among millions of Black people throughout American history who have suffered because of racial prejudice, it is also intended as a call for *all people* to be treated equally as brothers and sisters of humanity. The Vision contains words that resonate so far and wide and with such power that one of the evilest of all Vision Killers—racism—doesn't stand a chance. Dr. King may have been tragically gunned down, but his message endures stronger than ever nearly six decades later.

Zapping the Vision Killers

If you think your Vision is impossible to accomplish, view yourself as an artistic genius—at least in terms of Vision creation. No true Visionary—Pablo Picasso, Toni Morrison, Mikhail Baryshnikov, Virginia Woolf, Stevie Wonder, James Baldwin, Ernest Hemingway, The Beatles, Stephen Sondheim, Justin Bieber, Post Malone, Alicia Keys, Jennifer Lopez, or Maya Angelou, to name a few—would ever allow anyone (including themselves) to stop them from pursuing the greatest artistic achievement possible, even though their work likely challenged the thinking of their time. The most legendary artists achieved their status precisely because nothing held them back; they didn't care what anyone thought. As John Lennon once said, "Produce your own dream. If you want to save Peru, go save Peru. It's quite possible to do anything...."

Imagine the lesser impact Dr. King's speech would have had if he had directed it only to his children, his race, and his view of the country. Consider the Vision "I want to provide great service to those that I serve." It's clearly bigger than you and has altruistic benefits, but it's self-limiting. I suggest that it's an expectation, not a Vision. We should all serve those we commit to serving. Vision is something much more.

As you create your Vision, broaden its appeal to the most inclusive, expansive group possible. Imagine the massive potential of your flag being raised by people inside and outside your own tribe. And don't worry about whether it's too grandiose to channel the legendary Dr. King in devising and communicating your Vision. As famed acting coach Lee Strasberg once said, "If we cannot see the possibility of greatness, how can we dream it?" As an alternative, I would also suggest the following: "Even if we cannot see the possibility of greatness in a given moment, it should never limit us from creating it."

I hope you have taken this opportunity to expand on your Vision, make it bigger than you, and attach it to a cause or quest. Congratulations on your accomplishment—you have completed the first week of the Vision creation process. You are now ready for Week II, where you will learn how to collaborate with others to gain powerful allies and push your Vision over the top.

Remember one key takeaway that you will use over and over as you continue to develop your Vision. When a Vision Killer poses a challenge to you, always remember that Vision killing only lives in execution, which is a separate process. Therefore, be willing to say this phrase: "That point sounds like execution. Let's set that aside for now, come play with me in the Vision."

WEEK 11

You Must Successfully Collaborate with Others

KAT CLIMBS FOR CANCER BOY

A large, grayish cloud shrouded Mount Kallabore, foreboding a dark and menacing climb for Kat the next day. The 14,505-foot ascent had previously been accomplished by hundreds of mountaineers, some of whom had made it to the top without proper gear or even oxygen masks. Kat, however, had never attempted anything like this before and had some last-minute concerns, especially given the risk of bad weather.

Kat, an eighteen-year-old athlete, prepared weeks in advance of the climb by reading every mountain-climbing book she could find— particularly those about Mount Kallabore—and hiking several miles each day. The more she discovered about the risks and the questionable weather conditions, the more she realized it would be wise for someone to venture on the climb with her. She posted the following invite with a photo of the mountain in her social media feeds: "Looking for someone to climb to the top of Mountain Kallabore with me on July 10 to support my friend, Cancer Boy."

Katlin had initiated this climbing challenge to help raise money for a worthy Vision: the treatment of her friend, Tony, who had Stage 3 Hodgkin's lymphoma. Her initial efforts amounted to only a few monetary donations, which were much less than she'd hoped.

For Plan B, Kat solicited financial donations from her family and close friends, raising an impressive $5,000. Her father then introduced her to his boss, Mr. Block, who was president of his company. The executive was so impressed by Kat and her endeavor that he offered to personally match whatever was collected upon successful completion of her mission. Off to the side, he told Kat's father that he planned to match the donation whether she made it to the top of the mountain or not.

Kat's parents could barely contain their pride; their daughter was on the verge of accomplishing a major achievement. However, they privately shared with Kat that she had not followed through on her commitments to various causes in the past and hoped this time things would be different.

Noah, a casual acquaintance of Kat's back in high school, was scrolling through his social media feeds when he noticed her social media post. Since Kat was three years his junior, his memory of her had been that of a little girl—a tag-along with mutual friends. Not only was he suddenly taken by her attractiveness and how she had matured, but he was also deeply impressed by her commitment to such a noble cause. An avid climber, he'd read quite a bit about Mount Kallabore and had always been meaning to climb it. Now was his chance. He sent a message to Kat informing her that he was "in."

Kat was thrilled to have a climbing partner for safety—especially one who had some climbing experience—and to keep her company. The fact that it was Noah—on whom she had had a secret crush in high school—made it even more exciting. She confirmed with him right away and they made plans.

Kat awoke the morning of the climb consumed with doubt and fear, despite her training and the presence of a solid traveling companion. She called Noah and said, "I'm so sorry...I'm not ready for this. It's going to be a disaster. I need more time to train. Let's postpone for three months."

"Don't worry, Kat," he assured her. "I get that you're having second thoughts, it's natural. But I don't think you need the training.

I've read up on Mount Kallabore and am super confident we can get through it together. I'll have your back the whole time."

She sounded better but not fully convinced. "I don't know, Noah..."

"This is important for us to complete—for Cancer Boy. You already raised money and announced it," Noah asserted. "I'll tell you what. Let's start up the mountain and go as far as we can. If you have any hesitation, we'll turn right back. We're in this together. Okay?"

His voice had a calming effect, and his words reminded her of why she was doing this in the first place. Her attraction to him now seemed like much more than an old high school crush. "Okay," she relented. "You've convinced me. Let's go for it!"

They met up at the base of the mountain, checked their supplies, and began their ascent upward. To their pleasant surprise, the dark clouds were nowhere in sight, and it became partly sunny and warm with a light, cool breeze. They made great progress up the mountain, pausing only for a brief water break on a flat ledge with plenty of space.

"Thank you so much for responding to my ad," she said, having slurped down water from her bottle. "And for convincing me to go through with this. I'm glad we're doing it."

"It's for a good cause. Besides, it gave me a chance to spend time with you and 'hang out,'" he smiled, holding up air quotes on his last two words. For extra effect, he extended his right arm to make it seem as if he was hanging from a ledge.

She blushed at his choice of words to such an extent that she had to change the subject. "You know, my father's boss is going to match the $5,000 I raised for Cancer Boy."

"Really? That's amazing. Why didn't you tell me earlier?"

Kat shrugged. "No one besides you seemed very interested in this whole thing."

They made it to the top in half the anticipated time. The two high-fived their success, hugged each other, and even impulsively kissed before taking several photos of themselves amidst the beautiful scenery. They had so much fun that neither wanted to go back down...but, realizing they had no choice but to reach the bottom before sundown, they initiated their descent.

The pair reveled in their success over a pizza dinner. Now that she had a phone signal, Kat could post her pics in her social media feeds with captions like "Noah and me—on top of the world!"

"I'm so proud of you, Kat," Noah said. "You did it. Despite your second thoughts, you went ahead and accomplished your goal."

"I'd say we did it—together," she said. "But there's just one thing."

"What's that?"

"The $10,000 we raised is great—but Cancer Boy still needs another $80,000 for treatments. What good is the money if he's still not able to get what he needs?"

■ ■ ■

A few days later, Kat invited Noah as her "date" to attend a celebratory event in which Tony would be presented with a $10K check. Noah felt good about what they had achieved, but in retrospect, wished he had done more to help, given the $80K shortfall of funds. He thought about the old man who had advised him on Vision and wished he had met with him again. The old man knew many influential people and could have been a great resource to raise the fundraising bar.

Noah recalled something the old man had said to him just before he headed off to college. "Your first goal toward becoming a lawyer is to succeed in college. But you need a Vision, and you need to collaborate with as many people as you can, so that it can come true."

Noah realized that the old man's wisdom would probably have helped Kat's fundraising effort. While she had done a wonderful thing, the results might have been far more substantial if she'd recruited others in the collaborative effort right from the beginning. Noah had been brought in to help her climb, but he could have done more, helping her in her quest to raise as much money as possible. Noah wondered how many other instances in his life he had allowed a Vision or goal to lapse unfulfilled because he had not fully collaborated with others.

Chapter Four

Disposing of Self-Sabotage

To begin the second week, let's identify and resolve any self-sabotaging habits—whether in plain sight, behind the scenes, or even lingering in thoughts—that can upend all the hard work you've accomplished so far. It becomes a fool's errand to create your dream Vision Maker team and attempt to collaborate while limiting beliefs have manifested above or below the surface. And, yes, you must identify whether you are knowingly or unknowingly among the self-sabotaging culprits.

The Self-Sabotage Habit of Autocratic Leadership

The leader who touts collaboration and welcomes others into the group but is only doing so to make the process *appear* collaborative rarely inspires others. Whether intentional or not, this behavior exposes a leader who has autocratic tendencies, meaning she or he seeks power and/or control over others; does not listen to contributions from others; and overrides the opinions, recommendations, and counsel of advisors and team members.

When it comes time to brainstorm the Vision as a team, the autocratic leader—who regards collaboration as *support*, rather than *active participation*—ignores or shoots down ideas that challenge what has been created to that point. This is what team members hear: "I just wanted you to listen to my idea—not advise me on it. Your opinion means nothing. The Vision was done long before you stepped in the room." This approach has a countereffect, causing team members to become mistrustful and resentful; they feel as if they've been used, and their time wasted. The damage to morale can be far worse than if a Vision process hadn't been initiated in the first place.

Invariably, there are some autocratic leaders who flat-out resist the notion of collaborating with others and forming a team of Makers. They want their Visions to be *pure*. Whether they explicitly state it or not, they believe it's their creation and that other opinions would dilute and/or compromise it. A variation of this involves leaders who believe that other people would put up roadblocks and stand in the way of their Vision crossing the finishing line.

While there may have been a place for autocratic leadership in the past (such as former General Electric CEO Jack Welch), the complexity of today's society demands more from us. Younger generations eschew hierarchical structures and recoil when leaders bark orders for others to follow. They thrive on sharing ideas and information.

If you have any doubt about this, look at social media posts from users under age thirty-something. When you scroll down through the comments, you'll see myriad spins on the original post with fresh insights, ideas, stories, and images. They'll click Like or even Love, paste emojis, add links, and share the post with friends, who also join in. The original messaging morphs into something completely different as it passes through the chain, often with eye-opening results.

The spark that drives creative collaboration among Millennials and subsequent generations is precisely why you want them aboard the team. They will question everything, challenge the status quo, and ask the daring "What if?" questions the older generations wouldn't or perhaps lack the imagination to conceive.

That's not to say younger generations have it all figured out. They often leap to results without the benefit of experience that would lead to proper execution, which is essential to the success of any business. You can overcome this habit by simply repeating to yourself, "I welcome all ideas about the Vision."

Members of the Vision team need to be granted enough room to contribute. They also must be good listeners and allow time for other people to speak. That said, collaboration doesn't mean subjugating your ideas. Instead, all ideas are encouraged in equal measure and amplified when assembled all together.

Many leaders have blind spots when it comes to their leadership styles, which means I advise taking a good hard look in the mirror. If you suspect you give off even the slightest whiff of an autocratic leadership style, it's time for some self-reflection. Simply being mindful of how you react to other people's ideas—which may include subtleties in facial expression, body language, and/or verbal remarks—can help prevent being perceived as noncollaborative. You need to precondition yourself to *listen* to ideas from others and refuse to discount them.

Zapping the Vision Killers

If you have an itch to shoot down an idea from a fellow Maker during a Vision brainstorm session, simply state the following three words: "Tell me more." This allows you to take a breath, submerge the negative thought, and flip the script in your mind toward receptivity. It becomes an example of active listening, demonstrating to the team member that her or his opinion is *being heard* and *matters*. It empowers that contributor to feel comfortable and elaborate further and for others in the room to recognize that it's a safe place to contribute. The idea that follows may or may not be brilliant, but at least it has been given space for creative exchange to continue. Best of all, no one will think of you as an autocratic leader.

There is another potential hidden downside of autocratic leadership: recruiting congenial "yes people" who will give a thumbs-up to everything you propose. While you want energetic, positive people on the team, it's just as important that they think for themselves and say what's really on their minds.

By the same token, you don't want "negative Nellies" on the team who will hate every idea (especially ones that aren't their own), play political games (such as chronically agreeing with the leader to score brownie points), or leap straight to why a big idea won't work due to execution challenges. If you end up with just one such person in the group, meeting time will be usurped by everyone trying to appease her or him and nothing will ever get done.

The Self-Sabotage Habit of Lacking Self-Worth

Always keep this thought in mind: *You are 100% worthy of your Vision, so collaborate with confidence.* The self-deprecating story we often tell ourselves about our worth derives from our upbringing and the warnings that have been told to us throughout our lifetimes.

Below are just a few such stories that can derail us. As you read through them, think about which statement best reflects Kat's thinking in the story that prefaces this section.

> *You should finish what you started. (Maybe I shouldn't even start it.)*
>
> *We are responsible for the outcome.*
>
> *We must make it better or be quiet.*
>
> *We must have something important to say.*
>
> *We must understand before we speak.*
>
> *We must create ourselves first and then contribute and/or educate others.*
>
> *We must go through the hard knocks first before we can contribute.*
>
> *We must move further along on the journey before we contribute to others who are ahead of us.*

If you guessed the first statement, you would be correct! Kat has good intentions, but she expresses doubts about herself throughout the process, thereby limiting the potential of her endeavor. When she describes how her father's boss is going to match the amount she raised, she remarks to Noah, "No one besides you seemed very interested in this whole thing."

When you are looking to gain support for your Vision, you don't want to confuse humbleness with self-effacement. All Vision is worth sharing with others, and you need collaboration to take make it bigger, better, and more achievable. This is only attainable if the process resists judgment of any kind.

The Self-Sabotage Habit of Reluctance

Do you resemble most leaders who believe you are bothering or boring people by attempting to engage them—so much so that you barely even try? Are you like Kat, who went about her campaign so casually that she failed to generate much excitement? When you've attempted to create a Vision in the past, did you feel alone but didn't know how to lure others in your corner?

The self-sabotage habit of reluctance can be insidious, especially when it comes to approaching other potential Makers to support your Vision. Not only are you limiting the full potential of the effort, but you are also missing out on the joy of synergy from team collaboration.

I recently met with a delightful woman, Carina, whose passion involves helping people lose weight. "I love when they tell me I am restoring their life, including their ability to tie their own shoes," she said to me.

Carina's passion and Vision are well thought out, and her business is performing well. Despite her success, she confided to me that she was feeling tired and burned out. The cause of this hadn't occurred to her; she had been missing the camaraderie associated with team support and celebration. She'd been able to "get by" working alone. When I pointed out to Carina that the simple adjustment of working collaboratively would be more fulfilling, rewarding, and fun, her disposition completely changed, and she felt rejuvenated.

I've observed that many people who are reluctant to share their Vision tend to be extremely demanding of themselves. They often discount celebration, mumbling something along the lines of "I'll celebrate when the Vision is fulfilled." Collaborating on a Vision offers a ripe opportunity to celebrate a big win. This type of enthusiasm becomes contagious and generally leads to strong execution down the road.

The best approach when dealing with reluctance is to assume that people feel as you do and are always looking for ways to get involved in a promising endeavor. Consider adopting the mindset that, when you aren't sharing your Vision, you are cheating others of the opportunity to feel useful and relevant.

Reluctance can sometimes be a double-edged sword. Consider, for example, how you typically react when someone presents you with an opportunity to join a Vision process. Do you sigh, shrug your shoulders, and spew out a half-baked excuse for why you are too busy to participate?

It's inevitable that there will be occasions when being asked to join another person's Vision doesn't elicit tingles of excitement. You may indeed be overwhelmed with other initiatives and not have the time or mental bandwidth for it. You don't have to join every single effort, and in fact, you shouldn't force yourself to say "yes" if you lack the requisite passion and availability. However, you must still be willing to offer words of encouragement and thank the person for involving you in his or her dream. If your words or body language betray you, there is a good chance it will be the last time this individual approaches you for support. You can also rest assured this person will not respond well to you if you were to solicit him or her to support your Vision down the road.

Leaders need to be open in their thinking and be willing to collaborate, whether the initiative is theirs or someone else's. As you continue your Vision journey, remind yourself: "If it's going *to be*, it's up to *all* of us."

The Self Sabotage Habit of Failing to Empower Others

Have you ever been approached by someone who has a Vision that simply doesn't seem empowering enough? It triggers a feeling of uncomfortableness that is difficult to overcome. Your immediate instinct is a feeling of embarrassment for them—or sadness that they are chasing some effortless endeavor—so of course you want to avoid this person. I think most of us have experienced this dilemma at one time or another and can relate to it.

Let's go back to Kat's story. In her mind, nobody seemed to be paying attention to her Vision, so she simply announced it in a low-key fashion, which stripped away her listeners' ability to act on it. She needed to make her effort sound *bigger* without worrying about how people might react to a dose of hyperbole. Many more people would have climbed aboard her Vision if they were made more aware of the high stakes involved and that their support could save Cancer Boy's life.

If you have the right communication approach and empower people—which we'll cover in the next section—you don't need to fret about coming across as pushy and/or making others feel uncomfortable. You also shouldn't be concerned or discouraged when some individuals politely pass on signing up to join your Vision Maker team. Just as you've experienced, they probably have schedules packed with commitments and simply can't spare the time (at least at that moment). When they decline, thank them for listening and leave the door wide open, as you never know when they might change their minds or send someone else your way.

Busting through the Self-Limiting Habits

No matter which self-sabotaging habit has been blocking your collaborative efforts to propel your Vision, there are two concrete steps you can take to bust through them:

1. Focus on pitching the biggest aspects of the Vision. Do not dilute or undersell it.

2. Keep it brief, simple, understandable, interesting, light, and relatable. Think of it as an elevator pitch or as cocktail party conversation. Never pontificate or lecture. Choose your words carefully and state them with passion. Treat them as if you are describing your business or core product or service.

Let's take a specific Vision as an example:

To protect the elderly from abuse in care facilities.

How might you introduce this statement to someone in a social setting?

I would recommend launching the conversation with a general question such as: "Do you have an elderly parent or know someone who does?" This is a terrific starting point because the subject is universal. Everyone has either an elderly parent or knows someone who does. You'll therefore already pique interest, which opens the door to inserting your shatterproof Vision: "I'm passionate about making sure elderly people are physically and financially safe if and when they enter a care facility. I'm creating a mastermind group of people who share this sentiment."

This is a sensational Vision! No one could possibly contest it.

Prior to the event and your pitch, consider writing out how you plan to state your Vision. Practice it multiple times until it feels natural.

Once you've delivered the Vision, study the person's reaction. If she or he asks follow-up questions, it's a potential sign of interest in collaboration. It's also the window of opportunity to provide specific details on how the individual can get involved. At this point, you don't need to swoop in and push too hard. People dislike over-the-top, high-pressure pitches and are leery of committing to things that don't seem properly defined. On the other hand, you already have the fish circling the bait with an open mouth. Demonstrate your appreciation for the person's interest by inviting her or him for a coffee and idea-sharing session.

If the other party seems disinterested or distracted or changes the subject, it may indicate lack of interest. That's okay! It happens. It doesn't mean the Vision isn't worthy, or you won't find collaborators elsewhere. In any circumstance, it's rare that anyone will be put off when you share a strong Vision and properly deliver it.

To complete the first day of Week II, create a two-column chart. In the left column, note personal examples of self-sabotage you've committed. Go deep and be honest with yourself! Write freely and be specific about the problematic situations.

In the right column, craft a response to neutralize the bad habit. It can be a phrase, saying, or just a single word that will help trigger a different reaction from you. Once the lists are done, read them over several times aloud to establish awareness and to enable you to call upon the solutions any time you feel you are lapsing into a bad habit. It only takes a couple of days for your new, positive habit to become rote, and then you won't need to become as intentional about it.

Benjamin Franklin once famously said, "Who is strong? He that can conquer bad habits." As a historic eighteenth-century renaissance man and American Founding Father who accomplished Visions equivalent to those of one hundred people, he should know! He worked equally as well as an independent thinker, a leader, and as a team collaborator. He was a genuine Maker—often building his creations with his own hands—*and* a Visionary. He never let anyone—especially himself—sabotage his Visions, whether it came to brilliant inventions—such as bifocals, the lightning rod, the Franklin stove, and the flexible catheter—or other remarkable accomplishments, such as aiding the repeal of the Stamp Act and serving on the committee of five who drafted the United States Declaration of Independence.

Be like Franklin and enable your Vision to soar through good habits!

Chapter Five

Conquering Limiting Beliefs

imiting belief: a state of mind about yourself that restricts you in some manner. A limiting belief reflects an inability to see beyond your own experiences and often causes a pattern of stagnation.

We've all been guilty at one time or another of consciously or subconsciously holding onto limiting beliefs...

It won't work.

I'm not good at this.

I'll never finish this project.

I don't think I can take this concept any higher.

I don't have the time to figure it out.

What have been your experiences with the outcomes of the phrases listed above? Were they helpful in terms of saving you time and/or or effort? Perhaps limiting thoughts such as the ones cited caused you to put less effort into an initiative because you didn't see that they would make any difference one way or the other. Or maybe they led you to throw in the towel and drop the endeavor entirely, as you viewed resolving them as a waste of time. We form beliefs based not only on fears but also on results from our past experiences.

If presented with a choice, which would you prefer—the truth or usage of a limiting belief to protect yourself? Many of our limiting beliefs are not true at all, and yet we defend them in our minds as if they were real; the majority of these, unfortunately, tend to be negative.

To discover truth during the Vision process, we should remain positive that the outcome will turn out bright and successful. We discount limiting beliefs and place them on hold for the execution phase, at which point they will become invaluable as necessary challenges to overcome before they are given space to pop up later and bring down the initiative.

One thing is for certain: A limiting belief during the Vision Maker process rarely leads to a desired outcome. It increases the chance you will think in such negative terms that failure becomes a self-fulfilling prophecy.

Allison Maslan, whom I mentioned in an earlier chapter, has a brilliant expression: "Every level has a new devil." It happens she is specifically referring to the levels of scaling a business that are integral to the SCALEIT Method®. But I believe her statement may be applied to *any* new challenge and how your brain is wired to react to it.

I recently had a client, Ryan, who ran a shelving manufacturing company. He had a Vision to be the world leader in large box store shelving, offering unique mobile and efficient storage with unparalleled engineering. Ryan's company became profitable and grew so rapidly that it became a leader in the industry even sooner than expected. All good, right?

Once the company achieved its goals, the question naturally drifted to "What now?" When I proposed that it was time to reexamine his Vision, he replied, "I don't have time for that. I already know the recipe for growth."

Ryan focused so intensely on execution that his creativity froze. The outcome was a series of well-executed growth steps but with stagnant growth. Ryan's limiting belief—*my previous methods are the right ones and the only way to achieve even greater results*—brought the entire endeavor to a standstill. Worse yet, by refusing to even address the Vision, he was denying his team the opportunity to contribute to the business, which not only impacts their morale and sense of importance, but it also tightens the lid on beneficial ideas that could have led to business growth.

We'll never know what might have happened if he had chosen to suspend his limiting belief to see where the Vision Maker process might lead. Would it have resulted in a better outcome? I am confident the answer is *yes*. An outsider looking in who doesn't have the limiting belief has a certain beneficial optimistic detachment that shines a light on possibilities.

Limiting beliefs have dangerous consequences to us as individuals, but when they originate from the leader, multiply their impact by tenfold. Others soak up those limiting beliefs, and before you know it, you have a team lacking creativity and moving in the same patterns ever day until they burn out, feel frustrated at the lack of progress, and move on to something much more fulfilling. This ended up being the unfortunate case with Ryan's business.

On this second day, your task is to look with a certain detachment at opportunities available to you that you may not be seeing (or are attempting to avoid). Your limiting beliefs have shoved them aside and buried them underneath mounds of excuses as to why they would fail. Now is a chance for you to call them out and face them head on.

On a sheet of paper, create four columns with a heading for each:

1. A desired objective you didn't initiate.
2. A limiting belief about the objective.
3. What's *the worst* that can happen if the limiting belief about the desired objective is true?
4. What's *the best* that can happen if the desired objective is true and the limiting belief is false?

Take a few moments to jot down as many desired objectives you can recall that you didn't initiate. If you don't have at least three, you probably aren't challenging yourself enough. Next, in the following column, write down the limiting belief that prevented you from initiating the desired objective. In the final two columns, state the pros and cons of each desired objective.

When you look at the final completed table, I'd wager you will see that the upsides of the desired objectives outweigh the downsides—at least in terms of granting breathing space for a Vision to be created without any barriers and restrictions. Why am I so convinced of this? Simply put, most of the limiting beliefs are internal and based more on fear than fact. Human beings are wired to avoid tackling things that pose risk of failure, which sparks fear and avoidance.

Now that you have a greater understanding of how limiting beliefs may be "all in the mind," take some time to reconsider the desired objectives you scribbled down. Which ones are you willing to initiate with the dark shadow of limiting beliefs removed?

If you've ever been in a situation in which you let a great opportunity slip by due to a limiting belief, take heart in two facts: (1) it's extremely common to lose steam on an initiative at some point, and (2) the second day of this week covers how to overcome being trapped by limiting beliefs moving forward.

Positive Disruption

Years ago, I had a grade school classmate, Michael, who was a helpless daydreamer. During Math, English, Science, and every other class he would sit in his chair with his head lowered and venture off into his own world. Often, he'd scribble comic book stories and cartoons in his notebook from his active imagination. He loathed school and believed his only gift was drawing comic characters.

One day, our Math teacher called Michael's name out once… twice…*three times*…yet he failed to raise his head or acknowledge her in any manner, as his mind was so far away. Out of frustration, she screamed "*Michael!*" at the top of her lungs while hurling an eraser at him. The object struck his face, leaving a chalky residue on his cheek that was rather comical (at least to my classmates and me). What do you think happened afterward? Michael sat up and paid full attention!

Such behavior from a teacher would not be acceptable in our current society, and I don't ever condone a teacher (or anyone) launching any object at a student (or anyone)—even something soft and harmless, such as an eraser—but I share this anecdote to make a point. When you are in a mentally paralyzed state caused by self-limiting beliefs, one thing will jar you free from the pattern: an outside force, a *positive disruption*.

Let's look at a nonaggressive example of positive disruption. Imagine you are a writer working on a novel. Every morning at 7:00 a.m. you diligently sit at your laptop with a cup of coffee and start typing away, generally following your outline and notebook filled with ideas about plot, theme, characters, and so forth. You write for a good eight to ten hours each day, and after just three weeks, you find you are on a roll and already into chapter seven.

One morning, the flood of creativity draws to a screeching halt. You doubt everything: the premise, the story, the characters, the themes. You see plot holes and inconsistencies everywhere. You don't know if you should go back and fix them or continue to press on. You start to wonder if it's even worth it.

What if I can't get a publisher interested in acquiring it? And...even if I do, what if no one buys it? Worse yet, what if reviewers trash it?

You finally look away from the screen and realize that you've been staring at the same sentence for three days straight. During that time, you've deleted every word you've written seconds after having typed them.

Obviously, the above scenario describes a bad case of writer's block. What are the typical solutions for this common dilemma? Shake things up! I've helped several successful writer friends unblock, simply by disrupting their thinking.

My friend, Kevin, for example, is an accomplished lawyer and successful crime fiction novelist who has a way of lacing his stories with historical baseball lore and facts. During lunch one day, I casually asked how his third novel was coming along. He hung his head in frustration. "Jim, honestly, I think I've lost my desire to write. I don't think I can do it any longer. It hasn't been fun the past couple of months."

This jarred me because it was completely out of character for Kevin to speak this way. I perceived him as someone who loves to write and is quite good at it.

I suggested that he try a specific disruption (a term I didn't use): For one week, for a half hour each day, sit somewhere away from the keyboard. I advised him to handwrite freely—any thoughts on his mind—on sheets of paper with his favorite pen. He could write about characters in his book, his lovely wife, his career, observations—anything whatsoever. The one condition was that during this time he could not stop writing or even lift his writing implement. He was encouraged to ignore sentence structure, spelling, punctuation, and handwriting quality.

On completion of each daily writing session, he would place the pages in a manilla envelope marked "Musings." I made him promise that he would not review them before putting them in the envelope. In fact, he would *never* read them, as he had to discard the entire envelope at the end of the week.

Two weeks passed. I received a text from Kevin in which he thanked me for the suggestion. I received more details the next time we spoke. He had done exactly as we had agreed, and to his surprise, the following week he completed the most writing he had done in months. He became so excited and confident with his progress that he informed his publisher they could set a hard date for completion.

The point of sharing Kevin's story is to demonstrate how positive disruptions can break through limiting beliefs that are falsehoods. Kevin believed he was stuck and couldn't write his novel because his subconscious had convinced him of this fact. When he wrote freeform in a different setting without any pressure of having to complete something, his brain became liberated, and the limiting thoughts vanished.

Let's return to the limiting beliefs about the Vision that you are constructing. How do you cause positive disruption when you are stuck in a loop like Ryan or Kevin? How will you lead a team when they are stuck in a loop?

Perhaps another example will help you answer those two questions. Several years ago, I stumbled upon a nonprofit called CASA

(Court Appointed Special Advocate), which had been founded in Seattle and later opened a chapter in Orange County, CA. I was offered a position on the board of directors, which I accepted. I was by no means an experienced fundraiser or nonprofit board member, but I had enthusiasm for the cause.

CASA's mission has been to train and appoint a community member to be a friend to a child who has experienced abuse, neglect, and abandonment. The volunteer becomes a consistent friend in the child's life for the foreseeable future. In some cases, such as when the parents are in jail or temporarily stripped of custody, the advocate may be the only adult who consistently visits the child. The Vision is simple but powerful. Abuse is a pattern handed down from generation to generation, so adding a kind role model to a child's life disrupts the chain and prevents it from continuing.

At first, the Orange County CASA was solely reliant on community support. They met their fundraising goals by reaching out to several well-to-do donors who were pillars in the community, such as Carl Karcher (founder of Carl's Jr. Fast Food Chain) and Peter Muth (founder of ORCO Block Company). Both men were generous and loving donors, and they happened to devote some time toward mentoring me.

Unfortunately, during the CASA Orange County's early years in the 1980s, the aftermath of the recession strained nonprofit budgets. Large donors couldn't afford to support organizations at the same level as they had in the past. Both of my mentors said the same thing: "We are stretched this year, Jim."

Worse, they informed me from an insider perspective that most of their circle was of the same mind. It had all the earmarks of a lean donation year. I was concerned and reported this to our board.

To keep the organization afloat, the group had to figure out how we were going to raise funds from other sources. Previously, CASA had hosted a $100 plate dinner, but the suggestion of repeating the event didn't garner much support. Few innovative ideas were expressed at our meeting, and I admit I was a bit too intimidated at the time to speak up.

Although many Board members and my mentors were experienced professionals and excellent community leaders, they were stuck in the limiting belief that they only had two options for fundraising: solicit donations from large donors; or create another expensive rubber chicken/boring speaker dinner event that people endured, even though they hated it.

At the time, I was a young lawyer and didn't have enough contacts to "sell" a ten-person table at $100 dollars per plate. To my surprise, many of the other board members shared the same concerns. Given the economic environment and competing nonprofit dinners being hosted that year (especially by the much more widely known United Way), most of us had serious concerns about our ability to sell even half the number of required ten-person tables.

Just before the rubber chicken fundraising dinner concept was about to be rubber stamped, a fledgling member of the committee named Denise softly chimed in with two innocent questions: "What if...we *really try to entertain* people? Maybe people would be willing to spend more money?"

Denise's two questions threw some members of the board for a loop.

"We need to act now," one member snapped.

"We can't take the risk of a failed fundraiser," another followed.

As it happened, the proposed date for our event weekend coincided with the Kentucky Derby. I'd paid for much of my college tuition and housing by winning bets at horse races, largely thanks to a knowledgeable guy named Chuck—but that is another story.

During a lull in the somewhat heated debate, I summoned the courage to voice an idea: "What if we were to create a CASA Derby Day? Instead of hosting a dinner the night before, we could hold the event on the same day as the Kentucky Derby?"

I elaborated further, proposing that attendees would watch the Kentucky Derby together, dress up, make it fun, and we would attract more people with a low-price entry ticket of $20, since we didn't have to sustain the cost of the dinner.

The room exploded in excitement. I felt a tinge of embarrassment that I had been able to make such a welcome contribution. I would later be "thanked" by being appointed chair of the Derby Day committee (one should always be wary about volunteering a suggestion in a nonprofit, as it's likely you'll end up owning it!), an honor I was reluctant to accept at first, due to my lack of experience.

Ideas were thrown out fast and furiously. Fred Port, another stellar member of the community, mentioned that he had a connection with the Del Mar racetrack. He could obtain tapes of past races, which would be played for the crowd prior to the actual Kentucky Derby race. Attendees could bet with "CASA cash" on races from prior years—as well as those in the current Derby—with the payout odds all laid out. Winners received raffle prizes. We brainstormed creative food and drink ideas (such as mint julips) and—*voilà!* We had our new fundraiser.

The positive disruptor was Denise, who had posed the simple question on how we could create an event that would be "fun." During my stint as chair, virtually everyone participated in creation and implementation of execution because of the excitement sparked by the concept, which more than adequately offset my inexperience. We raised our fundraising goals *before* the event. On CASA Derby Day, auctions, CASA cash sales, drinks, and other activities contributed even more profit. CASA continued to successfully fundraise this event for many years.

Based on the above story, I would like to introduce an effective method for creating a positive disruption to help overcome a limiting belief:

1. Members should be encouraged to ask questions that challenge the group's thinking. "What if…"
2. The group should embrace the questions, offering creative answers to the "What if…" questions. Suspend the limiting beliefs—those tendencies that restrict our thoughts, including time constraints.
3. If you happen to be the primary leader, encourage free thought from all team members and eschew negativity.
4. Invite additional people to the group who are drawn in by the sudden positive energy of the refurbished Vision.

5. Once the Vision has opened the doors to creative thinking and development of a collaborative concept that everyone rallies around, memorialize the Vision and spread it far and wide.
6. It's time to commence execution of the Vision, which is effortless because there is an abundance of support and momentum for it.
7. The group can now collaborate to address and problem-solve any limiting beliefs that are genuine obstacles to accomplishing the Vision. The individuals who have held back their objections and concerns now have an opportunity to be heard, if they are not trying to derail the Vision (i.e., political motivations).
8. The initiative is a breakout success!

Now isn't that result a lot better than a rubber chicken dinner?

Facing the Upper Limit

In his book *The Big Leap*, Gay Hendricks coined the term *upper limit* in reference to the stress and fear people feel when faced with an uncertainty of the future. He proposes we should instead be happy because, when we become excited—rather than fearful—about a new opportunity, we become able to make a big leap forward. We know that feeling; things have been going our way for so long that we believe another shoe is about to drop, causing our world to fall apart. This is the human brain's way of protecting us from feeling too comfortable with success and taking our eye off the ball. When we attain a major goal that we truly wanted to achieve, we become even more vulnerable because we suddenly think we have something valuable to lose.

The upper limit mindset can be quite prevalent in all kinds of enterprises—both profits and nonprofits—which is why so many organizations get stuck. The mentality is that "We're doing okay, we're getting by—why change things and risk losing what we have going for us?"

Of course, if you ask yourself, "Do you really want to just be 'okay' and stay in the same place forever?" your answer will almost always be *No!*

The challenge is for us to find a way to suspend our upper limit thinking, while exploring the opportunities ahead. Gay Hendricks suggests you anticipate that a positive Big Leap is about to take place.

We often adopt a way of handling situations based on prior experiences, sometimes those we had as children. The "programs" we run are almost automatic. Often, I will ask a CEO, "When in your adult life have you taken your eye off the Vision or goal and suffered a great loss because you were not diligent?"

They are almost always able to share a story in which they suffered a loss. Upon further inquiry, they reveal that they had received warnings of the problem, yet didn't act on them. I follow up with another line of questioning: "Do you need to be fearful and operate under an upper limit—waiting for some failure to arise—or simply remind yourself that, when your diligence shows you a rising concern, you simply *need to act?*"

I share this narrative to encourage you to become your own mentor in this moment. Are you able to suspend your limiting beliefs?

Loralai owns a profitable business in which she and her team of thirty people collaborate to shelter women from their abusers. Unfortunately, Loralai struggled with the concept of upper limits for several years, until she finally confronted her demons. Internally, she battled against a deep, resonating anger; sometimes repressed, other times let out in a careful, metered way to her team. "My people are not following my clear instructions," she disclosed to me. "I fear they will let me down if I am not concise and diligent."

She sounded harsh in her tone, but I was certain she concealed the depth of her frustration when she communicated with her team. Clearly, she was conflicted. "I want to be positive, but when they do something incorrectly, I need to point it out to them so that they don't do it again."

Loralai had been raised in a loving family that was intolerant of mistakes. She had to overcome cultural challenges in which women were hindered from performing certain activities. This included running their own businesses.

As the years passed, Loralai's fear of making a mistake smoldered deep inside her, so it didn't surprise me that this emotion had inadvertently been starting fires arising from her management style. She was operating from a limiting belief: One fatal mistake was going to destroy everything she'd worked so hard to achieve. Her perfectionist attitude limited the company's creativity and ability to innovate and grow.

Zapping the Vision Killers

Have you ever spoken to an artist who loves to paint but refuses to share her work? Many (though not all) do so for one primary reason: They're afraid others will negatively judge their work. I would tell an artist (or writer) the same thing I've been sharing with you. Just create! Do it for your pleasure. Be truthful to yourself. Don't worry about the Vision Killers out there. Who cares what they think?

My mother happened to have been a terrific artist. What held her back was her inability to bring a work to closure. I saw the pattern repeat itself over and over. She'd keep fussing over each work, often painting over things that were beautiful but, in her mind, "imperfect."

After my mother's sixth iteration of a beautiful portrait of a rabbi she titled Fix—I don't know why she picked the subject, my family isn't Jewish—I grabbed it from the easel and declared, "You are done!" Fortunately, she listened to me this time and pronounced the work "complete." It's a wonderful thing, too, because the painting has garnered significant praise and inspired many people in the four decades since.

Perfectionism has its time and place if you are an electrician repairing a circuit, a surgeon performing brain surgery on a patient, or a proofreader scrutinizing book page proofs for typographical errors. When you are a business leader, you should expect mistakes and even revel in them, as they are excellent learning opportunities. They also present you as a transparent role model to the organization, allowing people to take creative risks without fear of harsh criticism when they admit to having done something wrong.

When I asked Loralai how she felt about her business and employees, she expressed elation about her company's profitability and what the team had accomplished. At the same time, she seethed about all the screw-ups, even though she believed she had always laid out clear directions for everyone to follow.

Loralai had to retrain herself to accept the fact that human beings make mistakes. By having allowed zero margin of error, she'd been causing at least three issues among her workforce: unnecessary stress and pressure, lack of learning opportunities, and restriction of creativity and innovation. If that wasn't enough, further investigation revealed that she was constantly barking out orders for others to follow without allowing them to ask questions or provide alternative solutions.

Have you ever told a child not to do something a certain way, yet they inexplicably went ahead and did it anyway? People (especially children) don't respond well to negatives. If I were to tell you "Don't think of a pink elephant!" what do you suppose will appear in your head (and probably has already)? A pink elephant, of course!

If you spend all your time searching for mistakes, it's guaranteed you'll find plenty of them. In fact, that's *all* you are liable to see—not insights and opportunities—as was the case with Loralai. Every mistake she discovered would confirm her worst fears. Her team became so fraught that they might get caught having done something wrong that they committed *even more errors*. Loralai had to face the irony that *she* had been the root cause of the mistake-laden culture all along.

A culture of confidence, however, encourages creativity and productivity. Once Loralai began to appreciate and change her limiting belief, her team responded. She was able to move from fearful to hopeful; her time suddenly became occupied by more enjoyable parts of her business, while she entrusted her team to take on more responsibility and handle day-to-day operations.

Address the Limiting Beliefs in Others

Pitching a Vision to someone with strong upper limit resistance can be quite a daunting task. It's easy to make a misstep, assuming someone will simply jump aboard and support your idea from the first verbal pitch. Imagine the resistance a naturally thin person will meet when she tells someone who has struggled all her life to lose weight that it's "easy." The dynamic changes dramatically, however, if the "seller" has firsthand experience with navigating the challenge and perhaps even personally conquered it. For example, back in the 1970s and '80s, slender fitness guru Richard Simmons pranced about and preached his exercise methods with tremendous success because he had the credibility of having shed 123 pounds himself through his unique program.

I've found that people who have broken through their own upper limit challenges can relate well to others who are still locked in that mode. This enables them to become advisors in a way, helping listeners inch out of their comfort zones long enough to realize that the Vision is safe and will, in fact, be a boon to their personal growth and development.

As a leader, you want to be conscious of your upper limits and learn how to program yourself to do it effortlessly. Once you've demonstrated to others that it's safe for them to also "let go," they will remove their own shackles and feel proud of what they are doing, rather than focusing on what "might" go wrong.

Storytelling can be an effective tool for communicating a Vision and its relevance in these instances, especially if the tale concerns you, is relatable, and gets to the point quickly enough. If you can provide the right amount of encouragement, you'll be able to help others realize that great things come from people who *embrace* their upper limits.

Consider for a moment tennis champion Serena Williams, who has won a record twenty-three Grand Slam titles. There may be a piece of her brain telling her that one loss from an upstart will destroy her status as the greatest and she'll be unseated from her throne. It's unlikely Williams would ever reveal her personal self-doubts (my guess is she doesn't have many), but my point is that no matter how many times she wins she always goes out on the court, match after match, believing she will perform *even better* than the time before. Wouldn't you like to experience even just a small a taste of Williams's success?

Now that you have ironed out your kinks, you are ready to move on to creating your Vision Maker team.

Chapter Six

Establishing the Effective Vision Maker Team

n the first few days of the second week, we set out to overcome the obstacles that might block or limit your Vision. These could be internal or external; known or unknown. For the balance of this week, we'll spend our time discussing the ways we find and attract the right team members. Once the team is established, I'll show you how to lead them for maximum results to enable your Vision to become the best it can be.

By now, I hope I've diffused the notion that creating your Vision is an independent exercise or that you're assembling the team to give credence to—or perhaps execute—a Vision you've already approved in your mind. There are many reasons why this would be a fool's errand, several of which I've already explored; since this is such a common pitfall, I'll reiterate them again:

1. Your Vision may not be grand or universal enough.
2. Your Vision may have missed something critical that a team member might catch.
3. If team members are left out of the Vision creation process, there could be resentment, and people might be skeptical of what you created—potentially leading to resistance, confusion, and/or morale issues.

4. The team members may have ideas you haven't considered that could take the Vision to the next level.
5. If team members are part of the process, they feel empowered and are more likely to be proud of it and become cheerleaders throughout the organization and even externally.

In short, imagine how rich your environment will be if you involve the team in the creation and elaboration of the Vision.

History Repeats Itself

I'm mindful of the repeated frustrations you've probably experienced from past Vision initiatives that went awry. No doubt you have at least a few battle scars and a graveyard full of Vision statements that perished quick and painlessly or suffered for years unfulfilled until they faded away and perished like unknown soldiers.

I'll bet the following scenario sounds familiar. You brainstormed the Vision, worked with an outside consultant or coach, sought counsel with your executive team, and maybe ran it by your significant other to confirm what you already believed: It was *perfect—pure genius!* Everyone assured you that "the team is going to love it!"

You arranged the Vision unveiling meeting with great fanfare, decorating the room with projection images, success charts, maybe even balloons and streamers. You laid out all kinds of delectable noshes and cold drinks on the table. After a brief introduction, you proudly declared the Vision to your team and handed out beautifully designed hard copies. At first, there were a few looks of mild confusion, followed by some blank stares, a few forced smiles—and then everyone applauded. A success!

The entire organization seemed to be on board…until later that day when you asked an executive team member how she thought it went. "Okay, I guess," she hedged.

"Come on, you must have *some* insight," you pressed.

She tightened her lip and replied, "Well, to be honest, their real reactions happened on their way out. I saw a lot of eyerolling and people looking at each other as if they were telepathically saying, 'Here we go again,' 'What a crock,' and 'This is total BS.'"

The next day, when you queried the entire executive team for information about why people didn't seem to be reveling in—or even discussing the Vision—they reluctantly admitted that they had seen their team members either discreetly tossing the Vision statement paper in the trash or burying it in their drawers. One manager commented that he'd overheard colleagues mocking the Vision in the pantry, stating: "It's going to be forgotten in less than a month, like the last one—why bother?"

A valuable way to rate the CEO's alignment with the team and organization is to randomly ask employees to state the existing Vision. In most cases, workers—including senior staff—laugh with embarrassment, admitting they can't remember a word of it—even if it's on the home page of the company intranet or on the wall of the front reception area. Those who attempt to reconstruct the Vision often botch a crucial word, demonstrating they never grasped it in the first place. Clearly, a new approach is needed—one that prevents all these potential detrimental outcomes.

Apply Marketing Principles to Create a Vision Maker Team

Vision creation requires a unified process that involves a collaborative and inspired Vision Maker team consisting of the right mindset, talent, creativity, open-mindedness, and dedication to the process. Once the right people are onboarded, they must be provided with clear messaging and direction, granted time and space to speak freely and candidly, and empowered to make decisions and take necessary actions.

To some extent, the process for recruiting people for this purpose is no different than when you are hiring and onboarding to join the organization. The role needs to be positioned as a mutually beneficial arrangement that is welcoming and has meaning for them on several levels. This can be a challenge, as current generations are looking to be involved in activities that come across as fun and educational, encourage collaboration and creativity, reject hierarchical structures, offer ample training and advancement opportunities, and provide a space for people to operate in their zone of genius. Most of all, whether it's stated or not, people are looking for purpose in any participatory endeavor.

If the above sounds something like a marketing strategy for "selling" something, you've read it correctly. A Vision team needs to be treated with the same respect as the organization's products and services, so it must encourage them to want to be part of something bigger. It also has to be made clear that the team will be armed with the necessary tools to create a magical Vision statement that is in line with the company brand and that will energize the masses both internally and externally.

Below are a few initial hacks that will make it easier for you to collaborate:

- Find a natural collaborator, enroll her or him in your idea, and encourage that person to help you.
- Don't think in terms of *your* idea or *their* idea. From here on out, you always refer to it as *our* idea.
- While collaborating, avoid discussing the execution. The *how* often stops the Vision in its tracks. You don't have to poo-poo or dismiss the *how* entirely; in fact, treat it as important, but parking lot it for when the Vision is complete.
- Find energy in speaking to others and identify people who share in that energy with you.
- Fight the urge to hide or obscure your Vision or suggest that you are revealing something that others will steal. That may be true on occasion, but more often, it's the opposite. If you keep it to yourself, and it never launches, everyone loses out.
- Collaboration should be *fun*! If you start to feel that talking to and/or working with a person is going to be *hard*, then it's not a good fit.

- Don't get too attached to any aspect of your Vision: Let the process breathe and direct where it should go.
- Treat obstacles as opportunities for inspiration and learning, not as attacks on your idea.

Lastly, before you get started on outreach, recognize that it should be a high bar to find people who will meet the qualifications for serving on the Vision team. This means you need to prepare for a challenging recruitment process. After all, you are about to create something much larger than your original Vision, which requires out-of-the-box thinking and an open-minded approach.

Creating an Avatar to Form the Vision Maker Team

If you've seen the James Cameron film *Avatar*, you already have at least some idea of what this section is going to be about. In the context of creating a Vision, an Avatar is a group of people with shared qualities and interests who may be grouped together around a common theme. Any gender may be an Avatar, but the titles "male" and "female" are too broad for our purposes. A topic such as "global warming" might be a suitable Avatar for a Vision in that specific space, but once again, it's too general.

One pitfall I've witnessed occurs when groups choose individuals who are all the same ethnicity (all Black, white, Asian, etc.). While they may serve as wonderful collaborators, they are limiting themselves to people who already understand, relate to, and agree with their Vision. What purpose does that serve? Instead, imagine the success they would experience if they were to broaden the candidate pool with diversity, but narrow the Avatar. The resulting Vision appeals to a much wider group of people who otherwise might not have paid any attention to it. People of diverse cultural backgrounds and experience might see blind spots and challenge a Vision that doesn't resonate among certain parties.

A female CEO client of mine—who happened to be a person of color—once openly declared, "I want people who are willing to strategize not just on diversity, but also fairness offered to *all employees* in the workforce." Guess what? Her Vision work succeeded beyond anyone's imagination *because* she recruited such a diverse mix of individuals.

Avatar Making 101

We're now ready to make our Avatar of a Vision collaboration team. On a sheet of paper, write down the Vision you developed in Week I. On this page, write "My Contacts." Underneath, list the names of people you know and respect who fit the criteria discussed above. Give some thought to everyone in the organization, as well as your circle of influence, and include those who might be low-key and fall under the radar. Sometimes, we overlook ideal candidates who are right under of our noses. As you carry out this exercise, you'll want to write down names of additional people who come to mind. Occasionally, a simple trait or value conjures certain people.

Often, I see people limit their lists to those they know personally. Instead of heading down this route, it might be worth identifying casual relationships or those you barely know but have personas or careers suggesting that they may be interested in your Vision work. They can always say *No*, but you have nothing to lose. I've found that high-caliber people are generally more than willing—perhaps even excited—to join a Vision quest that is powerful and aligned with their values.

On a second sheet, write "Avatar Traits" at the top and then the characteristics that describe the *type* of person who would be a suitable collaborator. Again, avoid thinking in terms of demographics. Your Avatar shouldn't concern economics, reputation, location, or ethnicity/race, but rather, areas of expertise, experience, and values that are essential to help create a Vision that is bigger than you.

It may also be beneficial for you to write down who *you* are; more specifically, list your values and traits. Use as many pages as you need. After all, you are passionate about your Vision, which says a great deal about you. These details—including relevant personal interests and/or where you see the organization headed—can help the group members understand where you are coming from and track with you directionally as you continue to collaborate. Be as expansive and specific as possible, clarifying your purpose behind the Vision. If they know *why* it's so important to you, they will identify with you throughout the process.

If you are struggling to identify Avatar traits, consider these thoughts:

- Create a list of benefits of the Vision, and then ask yourself, "Who is going to benefit from it?"
- Write down the skill sets you are looking for, as well as the job titles and descriptions that fit the bill.
- Identify the values that are of greatest importance to you. Who else do you believe shares these values?
- Brainstorm organizations that might be interested in partnering with you. If they share your cause and aren't in a competitive mindset, they might be more than eager and willing to supplement your efforts.
- Who will ultimately execute your Vision?
- Who has the means to fund your Vision?
- Who has the platform from which to amplify your Vision?

Don't exclude people because their interest in your Vision isn't immediately visible. Consider Kat's post on social media. She concluded that no one was interested because she hadn't received much of a response. This may or may not have been the case, but she'll never know for certain. What did Kat do wrong? She failed to embed a *call to action* in her post to fundraise and recruit others to help solicit donations alongside her, as well as make donations. Additionally, while climbing the mountain may not have been an activity of choice for some people in her community, they might have had ideas about how to reach other people they know who do have a relevant interest (such as a connection to a Facebook mountaineering group).

Imagine if she were to have also mentioned in her post *the goal* associated with her Vision and her *target date* by when it needed to be achieved. The specificity of a monetary request would have made her Vision seem tangible and pique curiosity—perhaps enough to have people follow her; monitor progress; hop aboard on a second, third, or fourth post; or just share it with their communities across multiple platforms. The deadline would have provided a sense of urgency and generated excitement, encouraging people to chime in and participate.

On a third sheet, write at the top "Where are my Avatars?" Jot down where these individuals reside, how they spend their time, what they read, and what interests and hobbies they enjoy. Are they located in the city, suburbia, beachfront, or the countryside? Are they in a physical workplace or working from home? What activities might they share: exercise habits; dining, shopping, and entertainment preferences; educational affiliations; hobbies; and so on? The better you can spell out *who* they are, *where* they congregate, and *what* their interests are, the greater likelihood you'll be able to pinpoint the most suitable people for your team and figure out how to reach out to them.

Include on these pages *how* your Avatars choose to absorb content. Are the desired people avid readers? Do they like books, blogs, magazines, or newspapers? Do they enjoy print or ebooks—or listen to audiobooks on earphones? Are they more visual, preferring web videos and webcasts? Are they engrossed in streaming video series? Hooked on video games? Do they update and scroll through their social media feeds every two minutes?

Spend some time drafting and reviewing your three lists. Don't feel this needs to be rushed in an hour. Take a few days to review and refine your lists. You may find some redundancies and overlap within the pages; in this case, you'll simply combine them to save space and make your list more cohesive. It's okay if you decide to rewrite a page a couple of times to get it right.

The final step is simple. On a separate sheet of paper, write "My Avatar." Look over your lists. Strive to create a simple but effective name that encompasses the essence of the candidates cited on the Avatar page, the traits that are calling out to you, their locations, and what they like to do and consume. Do not limit your list to one Avatar, your goal is to create four to eight.

An Avatar Example

Allow me to provide the Avatar for this book's purpose as an example for you to follow, starting with a Vision. Please note: Like you, I have my insecurities about the ability to promote this important Vision. As I've already admitted, I'm also a well-trained, instinctual, habitual Vision Killer. It's not that I've been sharing an untested process with you, I'm using my Vision as an example that will also promote the content of this book.

Below is my tightly defined initial Vision:

Encourage businesses to evolve from labor-centric to genius-centric profitability through a transformational way to build and amplify Vision.

I went through the Avatar creation process the same way I just outlined to you, filling out the three pages. I listed the people I know right now, those I met through others, and several I didn't have a relationship with but had a hunch they might have some interest. It ended up being a lengthy list, but it excited me to picture some of them as promoters and advisers to the Vision-building process—especially if they started out as Vision Killers.

I itemized the things I liked about their companies, careers, and interests. I researched where they hung out on social media, how they engaged with others, and even where they might be found. Lastly, I started plotting how I might attract them to a location where I could successfully interact with them.

I imagined my dream Vision-building team: those individuals who share my passions and goals and enjoy the satisfaction of helping others find ways to get unstuck—particularly when it comes to business revenue growth. I named one of my Avatars in this Vision project "the Coaching Expert, dedicated to client growth through Vision."

This is just one Avatar for my Vision team. There are many who aren't coaching CEOs but would love to impact the world through Vision.

The process is the same for you as you begin looking to establish language that represents your team. You can originate Avatars to help draw in candidates, or better yet, you can create a collaborative, highly integrative team to attract many different viewpoints.

Be playful while creating each Avatar. Think openly and get excited about those that could help you. At the same time, recognize that it's more important for the Avatar name to be described so accurately that the prospects and current team members are likely to say, "That's me."

I hope you feel the power of identifying the ideal Avatars and understand how critical it is to start a successful collaboration off on the right path. When you have suitable people on board the team who identify with the same unifying Avatars, they will put their hearts and souls into the effort and produce a Vision beyond your wildest dreams.

Crafting a Message That Will Attract Team Members

Now that your Avatar and collaborator traits have been identified, it's time to construct a message that will catch people's attention and compel them to join you. You've probably learned that the hardest thing about marketing a product or service is remembering the following three keys: (1) it must be congruent with the brand (or, this case, the Vision), (2) have appeal to the identified group, and (3) offer a compelling call to action. The sum of these three keys: The outreach must be *inspiring*. If you can't check off all these boxes, the effort will be a waste of time and money for everyone—especially you.

We are all overwhelmed with messaging we receive every day via technology: apps, texts, social media, and emails. Our work and personal lives have become intertwined in modern communication, which makes it even more difficult to wade through all the noise and spend time on the things that are truly valuable. Your messaging needs to rise above the cacophony, engage viewers' attention, and inspire the desired emotion. Otherwise, it will annoy people or blend into the background as just another trivial pitch.

Crafting the right message to attract people to your team requires substantial time, thought, and patience. You must adroitly "market" your idea to gain recruits. It's not to promote execution of a fully developed Vision, but rather, to share your work-in-progress developed in previous chapters and onboard suitable partners who can help you create something earth-shattering. At the same time, while the Vision you send out for this purpose is far from final, the copy still needs to resonate with the targeted audience. I won't attempt to repeat the content of hundreds of good books on messaging or summarize such a large collection of knowledge. If you stick to these basics, you will likely attract the Avatar you seek.

Passion Messaging

We know passion is a requisite, but sometimes we rush and draft language that speaks too directly to it before the recipients have had a chance to catch up and follow what we're talking about. A statement such as "I want to feed the world" is a passionate, bold Vision, but it's also an over-the-top cliché; it sounds like a personal Vision, not one that inspires others to suggest ideas or join, and might come across as unauthentic, overreaching, and limited to one person's Vision. It doesn't include the *why* or tug at the heartstrings. A more compelling message would be something along the lines of "We are forming a diverse advisory community to creatively discuss ways to irradicate hunger throughout the world."

Use your passion to enroll others in the Vision, but be careful to focus on the Avatar's interests and not just your own. This message is designed to attract the person who wants to participate in a discussion on world hunger. You want your message to solicit the response: "I share that passion." Write down any passionate messages you think you may want to share.

Fight or Flight Messaging

Our society has promulgated the idea that messaging always needs to be positive and upbeat. This need not always be the case as you fill spots on your Vision team. When utilized properly, fear can sometimes be an effective tool to trigger an emotional fight or flight response that will draw attention to your cause.

For example, if your team is promoting clean water, it's all right to state what might happen if the issue isn't addressed with a sense of urgency. Are there toxins or heavy metals in the water that might cause illness? By highlighting the issue in your messaging, you are eliciting a fight or flight response among the recipients, who might think: *Oh no, what might happen to my children if something isn't done to resolve this crisis right away?*

The "threat" may be on an even more individual level, such as countering pain. Julie, a product manager in a manufacturing company that produced office chairs, initially focused on positive messaging—low price and significant comfort—in her marketing messages. As it turned out, the chairs also reduced the risk of neck and back pain, which was foremost on the minds of many customers. Julie shifted gears and played off the potential pain and suffering the product prevented; as a result, sales increased, and customers became cheerleaders for her company's chairs.

On the same sheet of paper, write down all the fight or flight responses your current Vision messaging elicits. Next to it, itemize any pain relief or prevention your initiative addresses. When you're done, select your two most compelling statements. Boil the phrase down to one sentence that would inspire your Avatar to ask, "Yes, *how?*"

Below are a few examples of the negative consequences of inaction:

Want to share a seven second trick to stop heart attacks?

Protect our children from accidents caused by drunk drivers.

Create a program that protects against job layoffs.

Safeguard a teen from anorexia—a life in jeopardy.

Join us in supporting a way to prevent murder on our streets.

A Vision That Seems Logical...but Mysterious

Another approach is to appeal to the recipients' curiosity regarding a relevant issue. Many effective messages introduce an obscure fact, a future event, or a prediction in a way that is mysterious and immediately grabs one's attention. The ideal response is along the lines of "I want to know more about this idea" or "Tell me more." At the same time, the messaging needs to thread the needle and resonate as logical, so people will read it and say, "That makes sense."

Let's consider the following example from one of my clients: "What if we could reduce landfill use by half *and* protect the earth with one simple repurpose?" The mystery here is intriguing, allowing us think, *Wow, that would be amazing—how do they accomplish such a feat?* The gravitas to this pitch is that returned furniture can't be sold as new, so manufacturers throw it all in landfills. However, if some of this furniture could be reused, there would be a 50% reduction in garbage. This promise is mysterious and powerful.

If your Vision-in-progress inspires the question "Seems logical—but can it be done?" write down a fact, phrase, or idea that generates the curiosity without giving the answer. Next, answer the following prompts to broaden the appeal of what you have written. Remember: You are looking to *tease*, not delve into execution. The statements need to be brief and to the point.

- Does your Vision inspire people to change something in their lives—but there doesn't seem to be a way for them to see it?
- Ask a question that might elicit a curious response. Example: "Doesn't your dog deserve access to fresh water for twenty-four hours without fail?"
- Propose an ordinary solution and how it is cheaper, faster, and easier than any other alternative. Avoid mentioning the features that provide the solution. Here's a simplified example: Nike's image of an athlete doing something incredible, accompanied by the words "Just do it."

Below are some logical but mysterious pitch statements to help you refine your pitch:

What will your children drink if water is no longer plentiful?

How will we continue to innovate in technology if we no longer have Internet access?

Would you prefer your husband present you with a creative gift or yet another flowerpot for your birthday?

Are you all right with music being removed from your child's school?

Avoid Words That Trigger a Snap Judgment

Let's suppose your Vision professes to elevate and excite the process of buying a car. The current iteration of your Vision proposes the following: "Would you like to help innovate an exotic car buying experience that excites a potential customer?" The problem in this example is the choice of the word *exotic*. While the word might sound intriguing, it also has several unintended connotations that might cause your Avatar to scroll past it; in addition to meaning *exciting*, it can also imply *unusual, uncommon, out of the ordinary*, and *rare*. It could even be off-putting because the average buyer may not care about the buying journey of a $275,000 Ferrari, yet they may have profound insight on your team. If you don't want people to misinterpret your messaging, consider replacing the word in question with something more direct that appeals to an emotion. For example: "Join us in developing a *fun* car buying experience."

Other words that elicit emotions are typically laced with undercurrents of popular or unpopular subjects or reactions. Don't use slang, which is often associated with several meanings, and for a lot of people, it can be derogatory and unappealing. Consider these subjects and words, all of which convey a sense of adversity: derogatory phrases, judgments about others, segregating phrases or words that are intended to divide us by natural traits, disability, underground, cover-up, secret or hidden agendas, censorship, manipulating, scandal, unstable, wicked, corruption, rebellion, and alienation. While many of these are used in advertising to elicit a response, I recommend you stay away from them when trying to attract people to support your Vision team.

Zapping the Vision Killers

Recruiting for a Vision team is a two-way street. While you want smart, talented people who match the team's various Avatars, you also need to be on the lookout for individuals who have a hidden agenda or may have a naysaying workstyle or are unable to sit in a discussion without popping the balloon. In more extreme circumstances, you may encounter someone who is intentionally looking to sabotage the Vision before it can get near the launching pad. The fact is that there are some people who are going to attempt to shoot things down, no matter what. A few of them may be gifted at being manipulative and crafty, submerging their true intent during early discussions and seeming positive and upbeat. Then, as soon as the process moves forward, they are angling to raise their objections behind the scenes to demotivate other team members.

You need to prevent this at all costs. When you are recruiting, how do you identify this trait before it's too late? Like any interview process, ask new recruits for specific examples of previous collaborations on teams. An obvious sign is if they struggle to come up with one. More likely, however, it will be revealed through statements such as "The team never listened to me," "The team had bad leadership," or "I ended up having to do everything myself."

Another tact is to propose a scenario in which the candidate spots a glaring problem with the Vision while it's being developed. Ask her or him the following: "How would you handle this situation?" If the recruit replies with anything that smacks of "I would speak up right away and make sure we fix it before we waste another second," you have pinpointed a professional Vision Killer and should enlist her or him to do one of the following two roles: agree to suspend the Vision killing while the Vision is developed, leaving the objection for later; or ask her or him to be on the execution team after the Vision has been created. If the person can't commit to one of these options, move on to the next person.

It's good practice to look at each word in your messaging from a different angle. How else might it be interpreted? In this day-and-age, you need to be especially careful not to slip into any sensitive area that may inadvertently offend someone. Even major advertisers have blundered on occasion with inadvertent off-putting language and/or imagery. Pretzel Crisps once ran an ad campaign with the irresponsible tag line "You can never be too thin," which rankled people who have been impacted by anorexia, as well as those that who feel criticized for their size. Sometimes the misstep is a result of misdirected humor, as in the case of Reebok's epic fail with this ad: "Cheat on your girlfriend, not on your workout." Oops!

Finalizing the Message

Congratulations! You've already devoted more thinking about how to form your Vision team than most leaders. Now it's time to wrap this up in a clear, crisp message that will captivate potential recruits for each of your Avatars. Some messages will work for all of them; others will be more specific to that Avatar. Familiarize yourself with the best for each and choose the right one when reaching out to each Avatar candidate you selected to approach.

Go back to your three columns and your conclusions. No doubt, numerous sensational ideas are already percolating. If not, don't worry! It doesn't have to be a fancy, flashy, and hype-filled saying—although if you have an exceptional one, use it! The goal is to achieve authenticity by evoking fight or flight, creating a mystery, or trying to elicit an emotional reaction. You want to craft your message several ways, each time using one or more of the three categories, and it may be slightly different for each Avatar type. In my case, I've targeted coaches as well as brilliant CEOs for my Vision team.

The coaches will be more moved by messaging that taps into their coaching experiences, while the CEOs will be more interested in the messaging suggestive of their real-life, practical business experience. Both Avatars will want to forward the Vision, but the messaging will attract them differently. Below are a few examples of various messaging categories. You can elaborate on each one for the respective Avatar you've created.

Water should be a given right for all children. (Emotion)

Kind and safe care for our elderly is not a goal, it's an imperative. (Curiosity)

Availability of U.S.-made microchips protects our country from foreign governments stealing our market share. (Fight or Flight)

Ice cream should be pleasurable and not contain unhealthy ingredients. (Fight or Flight)

At this stage, you should have enough direction to construct four to five solid messages. Test them out on a half dozen trusted, objective people to determine which one will rise to the top. If the results are evenly spread out among the options, make your best judgement call.

The Three C's: Congruency, Consistency, and Call to Action

You are officially in the home stretch of creating your messaging: the refinement stage. I've devised the three C's—congruency, consistency, and call to action—to help lead you to final language.

Congruency

Congruent is a fantastic vocabulary word you might have picked up way back in grade school in your Math and/or English classes. As a reminder—and to save you the trouble of Googling it—the word means "equal" or "in harmonious agreement." While troubleshooting your statement, you want to ensure that your promise matches up with your intent and rings true.

How do we recognize if our messaging is incongruent? What if we are so close to it that we can't tell?

I'll let you in on a little secret: We all have a powerful subconscious mechanism for knowing things we shouldn't really know—our *intuition* or *gut feelings*. This is when something doesn't feel right, even if you can't put your finger on what it is or why.

Imagine you are seated on a train when a despondent, teary-eyed woman with a backpack appears and addresses the travelers: "I'm so sorry to bother you, but...I need to get back home to my family... and my wallet was stolen. I don't have enough money for the train fare. If you could find it in your heart to spare a dollar, I would be most grateful."

Several passengers feel sorry for the woman and hand her a dollar. You are about to reach for your purse (or wallet) but then pause. Something feels off to you about the woman, but you just can't put your finger on what it is. Your gut is telling you *there's something fishy here*. You let the woman pass without giving her any money.

One week later, you are once again aboard the train and guess who materializes—the same woman with the backpack, her face just as low-spirited as the previous time you saw her. "I'm so sorry to bother you," she begins, "But I need to get back home to my family..."

You know exactly where this script is headed and realize that your intuition had informed you something was incongruent about this woman one week earlier. Your gut saved you from wasting your hard-earned dollar on a fraud.

Think about whether your messaging intentions are properly aligned. If your messaging is incongruent with your Avatar, revise it or strike it off your list.

Let's suppose you are the CEO of a company that manufactures and installs recreational equipment for indoor and outdoor play areas for young children. Your messaging reads: *Towns that build beautiful and safe play areas for kids attract and retain great residents. Help us to transform your community by installing our monkey bar set in Walker Park.*

What do you think is wrong with the above statement? If you answered, "Some people believe monkey bars are dangerous and cause injuries," you would be 100% correct. Some parents shudder at the thought of their three-year-old taking a fall from monkey bars. The word "safe" in the prior sentence alerts them that the initiative is potentially incongruous and, therefore, unauthentic.

Consistency

We must make sure we are consistent with our messaging. One of the biggest marketing failures is a lack of consistency in the advertisements. Consider this typical advertisement technique to demonstrate the point. "If you are not completely satisfied, we offer a written money back guarantee." Yet as you search through the fine print, there is no written guarantee. You will move on and so will your Avatars if your messaging is not consistent from start to finish.

Consistency does not constrain the various features and benefits of your Vision. We simply want to make sure we are fully explaining the elements that attract the Avatar to the Vision, leaving them excited to move forward rather than curious or confused. Identify the particular interest, and then focus on fully outlining how the Vision supports that interest. Present questions and be curious about feedback. Many times, the Avatar will answer their own questions.

Often we get so excited about the many benefits of our Vision that we continue to laundry list them and the Avatar loses interest or feels a bit overwhelmed. Just remember, you have spent a lot of time thinking of your Vision. Be patient while your Avatar gets up to speed.

Call to Action

Every marketing strategy must involve a call to action, one that encourages people to say *Yes* as an immediate reflex. As we all know, this is easier said than done. People tend to refuse solicitations of any kind that are off the cuff. We train ourselves to say *No*—even to a query from someone we know and trust—simply because we already feel overwhelmed and unable to take on one more thing. The greater the perceived commitment, the more anxious recipients will be. If a pitch is longwinded or in any way confusing, you can rest assured the response will be a terse "Thanks but no thanks" (if there is any reply at all).

My experiences indicate that sometimes it can take several years to gain traction for commitment to something ambitious. For this reason, your messaging needs to consist of a *series* of calls to action to achieve the maximum result.

I often like to discuss my client's actions in terms of dating, as almost everyone can relate to it as an analogy. Meeting someone for the first time requires patience. Few people ask someone out on a date during a mere introduction, as they recognize the chances of success are minimal. Physical attraction can only go so far. We also need to know a little bit about the person and determine if we like and trust him or her.

For this reason, when we are developing a call to action, I recommend that we grant the person on the receiving end of the messaging some time to process the pitch and warm up to it. Like dating, *like* and *trust* must be *earned*, which means we need to exercise patience. Being too pushy and aggressive will generally frighten the fish away from the bait.

Your primary goal, therefore, is to start by proposing a *minor ask*—not a full-fledged commitment. In doing so, you offer an opportunity to learn about each other and determine if it's a reciprocal good fit. To continue the dating analogy, you can "go for coffee" instead of jumping right in with an invite to dinner at a fancy restaurant.

In terms of recruitment, this translates to creative ideas such as the following:

- Create a slideshow or a video short.
- Set up a "Vision Killer review." During the meeting—which can be virtual or in-person—you present your pitch live and then ask, "What do you think is wrong with this Vision?" In this way, the candidate becomes immersed and invested in the project and feels as if her or his opinion is valued—especially since you are putting your Vision in the vulnerable position of soliciting feedback.
- Chat over a (literal) coffee meeting.

- Design a simple (one page) flier for candidates to review.
- Conduct a short 1:1 verbal survey. People love offering their insights and opinions.
- Invite potential recruits to a group meeting or mastermind, which will provide some insights into the project and existing team culture without asking for a major investment of time.
- Organize an expert discussion on the topic with the candidate.
- Engage the other person with simple questions: "How does the current Vision make you feel? Does it inspire you? Does it make you feel sad or happy?"
- Invite the individual to share an idea on how the Vision might grow even larger.
- Find out as much as you can about the other person, and ask what she or he would want or expect to hear regarding the Vision.
- Ask for a $1 dollar gift; in return, you can provide an inexpensive gift (such as a bookmark with the current Vision designed on it).
- Post a suggestion box in an accessible spot; anonymous contributions sometimes help shy people come forward when they feel respected and safe.
- Create a Frequently Asked Questions list.
- Find a link between the recruit's business and your Vision. If you can make a connection on that level, you'll have an easier time explaining your Vision and demonstrating its value.

Armed with the above tips, you have plenty of options for determining a call to action that works for your outreach. For now, on a sheet of paper, identify a series of at least three calls to action; each should be a gradually escalating commitment for joining your Vision team.

Be Realistic about Response Times

If you don't hear back right away from people, don't assume—like Kat in the opening story—that there is a lack of interest. As we've already established, people are super busy and inundated 24/7. They may not have had a chance to scroll through their emails yet or are simply allowing some time to think about it. An email may also end up in a spam folder, so it's a good idea to ask for an email confirmation on receipt.

Mindy, one of my clients, created unique and delicious ice cream sandwiches. She made several attempts to distribute her product in a chain of stores and finally managed to set up some time with the buyer. The meeting seemed to go well, but afterward she heard crickets. As weeks went by without any kind of response, she leapt to the conclusion that the buyer wasn't interested and was about to give up.

"Don't assume you know what's going on. Just wait it out, you never know," I encouraged her.

She followed my advice and patiently waited another week. Still nothing.

"All right, I agree this is getting frustrating," I conceded to Mindy. "Enough time has gone by that I think you can reach out to him—but without any kind of pressure or annoyed tone. All you have to do is ask, 'Are you okay? I haven't heard from you and hope all is well.'"

She followed my suggestion. To her amazement, it did the trick. The buyer called her and apologized profusely. "I'm fine—and I'm so sorry for the delay. We're really interested but I've been so overwhelmed recently...."

Never assume you know what the other person is thinking or going through when you don't hear a response. While it is possible for you to intentionally be ghosted on occasion, you don't know that for sure until you have waited it out as long as possible and tried out my "Are you okay?" technique.

A Few Words about the Medium

Lastly, you want to deliver your message in a medium that is acceptable for the content. An invite to a Zoom meeting or a telephone conference is perfectly fine, as is an email with documents and graphics as attachments.

There are two cautions, however. The first is to avoid sending anything too wordy or attaching large files. These days, sending a PowerPoint attachment is a big no-no, as the software is considered a bit passé by some people, and the file sizes can be enormous and clog up inboxes.

The second caution is to be careful to avoid too much hype in the subject line, as that can be an immediate turnoff (or cause the message to get dumped into spam). Utilization of all capital letters and exclamation points are also tip-offs to a heavy-handed pitch.

It goes without saying that the *content* of your messaging is far more important than the delivery method. This becomes an even more pressing issue as we head into Week III of the program and seek to spread your Vision throughout the galaxy.

Once your team has been enrolled, open the floor to discovery and refinement, and provide the necessary encouragement to postpone any Vision-killing statements. You will oversee the process, allowing the magical combination of creative discussion and teamwork to engage the participants.

Now you will discover how big your Vision can truly be!

WEEK III

Evangelize the Vision to the World

THE OLD MAN OFFERS A NEW LESSON

The years passed, during which time Noah and Kat wed. He completed law school and landed a job at a prestigious law firm, while she became an instructor at a high-profile climbing club. The happy couple lived in a beautiful three-bedroom house and enjoyed bouldering together at least one weekend a month.

Whereas Kat excelled at her job and loved it, Noah became restless. He couldn't quite pinpoint what else he wanted. He enjoyed helping his clients and was rapidly moving up the ladder at his firm. He considered buying a larger house someday, but the idea didn't feel satisfying. He seemed to be going through the motions of trading his time for more money and purchasing bigger, more expensive things that left him feeling unfulfilled.

One day, Noah awoke with a desire to return to Mexico and visit the old man and the other people he had met as a teen. "I need to figure this out," he told himself, hoping the trip would provide some answers.

While in Mexico, after visiting with friends, Noah and Kat asked around for the old man. They found his daughter, who said, "He is sitting on the stump by the lake, as always." Jogging his memory, Noah led his wife on foot toward the lake. He looked forward to introducing his new wife to the old man.

It didn't take long for them to find him sitting on a familiar stump, the same one from which he had counseled Noah before he ventured off to become a lawyer. He had struck Noah as old many years earlier, but now appeared to be a centenarian. Despite the wrinkles, lost hair, and shriveling frame, his eyes remained as clear and piercing as ever.

The old man recognized Noah right away and was pleased to see him but was more intrigued by the woman accompanying him. He grasped her hand and asked her name.

"Kat," she replied.

He seemed perplexed.

"Gato," she translated.

The old man produced a laugh so hard it seemed as if it might cause his body to crumble. "You are a cat, are you?" he wisecracked. "What do you like to do, young Kat?"

She filled him in on her passion for climbing and teaching.

The inevitable question followed. "What is your Vision?"

"Oh no," Noah muttered.

Kat leapt at the opportunity to explain that the original purpose of her climbing had been to provide financial resources for a sick friend. Since that time, however, she had come to love the sport, and teaching allowed her to help those who wanted to overcome their own limitations and fears. She next expressed something Noah had never heard before: "I want to create an instructional school that teaches adults, teens, and children to overcome personal obstacles through climbing and mindset education."

The old man nodded to Noah to signal that he had chosen his partner wisely and then readdressed Kat. "And what are you doing to share this Vision with the world?"

Noah felt a bit left out. After all, the old man was his mentor and friend, and he had expected to be the one to garner his attention.

"I haven't told anyone about my dream yet," she confessed. "It doesn't seem like the right time."

The old man released Kat's hand and announced to them both, "You are a fine married couple. You are on the journey of Vision Making together—how wonderful!"

The old man didn't ask Noah how his Vision had been maturing. Instead, he began to reminisce about the Pitaya business he took over as a young teen in his hometown, Ejutla. "Pitaya is a rare cactus fruit that must be picked at exactly the right time, or it is useless, sour, and hard or rotten. The picking window is so narrow that large-scale cultivation in a tiny community such as Ejutla is difficult...."

The old man went on to inform them that Pitaya had been the town's livelihood for more than a half century. A Vision had been shared and adopted by the entire town, passed on from one generation to the next. Despite the myriad challenges of harvesting the fruit, Ejutla figured out how to produce it with enough efficiency to sustain the community.

The old man paused for a moment, his eyes burning into Kat's. "Do you think it was possible for the people of Ejutla to continue this Vision alone?"

Kat shrugged, dumbfounded.

The old man mimicked her shrug and blared, "No, no, no!"

She recoiled as he continued: "We needed to share our Vision with the world and do it in such a way that people would be eager to support us. We created the most famous Mariachi festival in Mexico. People came from all over the world to hear the wonderful music. It happened that we also sold them Pitaya, which are ripe at the exact time of the event."

His gaze wandered off toward the massive lake. With a lowered voice, he said, "A Vision must be bigger than you. Others must collaborate with you to help create it. Most of all: For a Vision to be fulfilled, it must be shared with the world."

Chapter Seven

Enrolling Others through Temperament

Welcome to Week III! I suspect that you, like Kat, have conceived an idea or even developed a full-blown Vision at one time or another yet never shared it outside a select group of people. Think back to that experience. Do you recall how you felt about the notion of sharing it? Relive that sensation for a moment. If you are feeling intense discomfort, I'm probably correct in assuming you didn't press forward because you thought you might be judged, were afraid of how others might react, were uncertain of how to get it done, or lacked enough confidence in the Vision itself.

At this juncture—the start of Week III of the program—you must be certain of these four irrefutable truths:

1. Your Vision is powerful.
2. Your Vision is worth sharing.
3. You are more than up to the task of spreading the word of your Vision.
4. If you do not use every means at your disposal to enroll others in your Vision, it won't live up to its full potential.

Are you wavering even the slightest bit on any of the above four truths? If so, return to a childlike state of mind. Imagine you were a six-year-old artist who completed her or his first painted masterpiece.

Wouldn't you unthinkingly trumpet your horn to everyone in your vicinity and coax them into admiring your work?

Be uninhibited, be bold, and be confident with your Vision. If you don't, no one will be inspired enough to climb aboard your bandwagon or be able to hear it above the fray of so many others simultaneously clamoring for public attention.

To share your Vision with the world, I would like to suggest opportunities where you'll find great support. Don't worry, we'll handle temperament in good time...

- Your Vision is attractive to your ideal client, so consider presenting your product, product name, packaging, and message to this individual or entity.

- Your service may be framed by conveying your Vision not only to those you have already been identified as users of your services but also to those people who *know* others who may want or need those services.

- Consider letting your Vision infiltrate your organizational hiring and your employees. Once it is introduced to the organization, you become able to build culture based on the ability to unify everyone to the common goal.

- Wouldn't your customer journey be a perfect opportunity to announce your Vision—not just verbally but also building it into the fabric of your customer's experience?

- Imagine a cocktail party conversation in which you are asked what you do for a living. Would it be ideal if you shared your Vision with the other interested party, who then asks you to explain it more? Suppose you were to say, "I make sure Ugandan children have fresh drinking water, and we do it effortlessly for several generations." Who wouldn't then ask, "How do you do that?"

- Consider preparing your ten-second elevator speech in which you introduce your Vision, encouraging others to ask *how* or *why* questions. Of course, imagine discussing the Vision from onstage, in a book, on social media, with your community, at a church event, or even when having fun with your friends.

You can see that the above is by no means a comprehensive list; however, it is enough to get you thinking. The primary concern is managing the enrollment and temperament of others who will share your Vision. I promise that, if you pay particular attention to this next section, your Vision will become a reality far faster than if you were attempting to conquer the world alone.

Managing Temperament

As you are now being tasked with sharing your Vision with the world, you must also manage the temperament of your organization and yourself. I don't mean to imply that you or anyone "has a temper" (meaning, easily triggered and angered) or lacks enough enthusiasm in general. Rather, I've observed three potential ways the wrong type of temperament might interfere with the team's ability to announce the Vision to the world and garner support for it:

1. The limiting beliefs of certain individuals.
2. A lack of conviction behind the Vision.
3. The leader failing to engage in the Vision-sharing process.

Let's address each of these individually and determine how to prevent them from becoming issues in the first place.

Anticipating the Limiting Beliefs of Others

In the first two weeks of the program, we spent a great deal of time establishing how to ensure that the Vision Makers remain in a Vision

Maker space throughout the early stages of the process. The same remains true as you begin to unveil the Vision to the world.

You will encounter at least three types of personalities as you and other supporters present the Vision: the naysayer, the eternal optimist, and everything else in between. You must prepare yourself in advance for every potential response to keep your Vision alive.

First, recognize that it's impossible to be everything to everyone, and no matter how hard your team tries, you won't please all who hear your Vision. Right out of the gate, there will be some workers in an organization—especially those who are already unhappy and have an axe to grind—who will either privately or publicly despise anything you bring to their attention. Some of these individuals are just hardened skeptics; others are wired to destroy what people worked hard to create; and the rest have a soured relationship with leadership or the organization itself (and probably should head to the nearest exit).

My advice? Don't spend any time worrying about them. As studio executive Bonnie Hammer once said, "You can't change how people act, but you can change how you react."

The Avatars you created in the last chapters will help you overcome the limiting beliefs of others. You will work together to broadcast the Vision to all current and potential future stakeholders.

Your Vision Maker team is now ready to work together to prepare a list of potential objections that will most likely be raised the moment the Vision is shared. You can be certain that 99% of these will be related to execution. This is to be expected, as it's our tendency as humans to react logically and realistically. The immediate reaction from well-intended people is to think only in terms of *what is possible to accomplish today*; they only see the obstacles, not the big thinking that went into the Vision-Making process. This is all okay.

By the same token, you couldn't possibly answer all execution problems in your Vision communication, so don't even attempt to do so at this stage. What your team *can* do, however, is identify the legitimate objections and questions that are bound to arise and have a working idea of how to approach the discussion, while also overcoming the conclusion that the objection is an insurmountable problem. By being transparent and acknowledging awareness of the concern upfront, you are preventing individuals from trying to make it seem as if achieving the Vision isn't grounded in reality and, therefore, is impossible.

Consider the following Vision: *We are going to create a new category of consumer cleaning products that reduce exposure to harmful enzymes and are safe for humans and pets.*

Below is a likely objection: *How are we going to get this done?*

The exact method of executing this Vision may not yet exist, but that doesn't mean it isn't achievable. In anticipation of the objection, you might have something like this in your back pocket: *We've successfully achieved this for industrial cleaning products, and with some effort, I believe a good portion of that technology will be applicable here.*

Zapping the Vision Killers

Your team's list of objections might be one page or a dozen. No matter how comprehensive your list ends up being, there will still be those who try to show how smart they are and poke holes in the Vision. Expect that at least one person will pose an objection that no one considered. When that occurs, praise the individual, accept the comment, and state that it will be added to the list of issues to be resolved in the execution phase.

The main consideration is that your team identifies and presents the objections in a way that nurtures the proper receptive temperament of all current and future stakeholders. By seeing that the Vision Maker team intends to address all objections during the execution phase, individuals will learn to trust the process and become receptive to the Vision itself.

Communicating with Conviction

You're probably wondering why I've singled out *communicating with conviction* as one of the potential issues you'll face when it comes to temperament. If you and your team display the least bit of doubt when presenting the Vision, others are sure to pick up on it and feel it's not worthy.

The first way to build confidence is by recognizing that there is power in numbers. You haven't been alone in this journey. You've had the benefit of a gifted Vision Maker team that enabled you to think bigger than anyone ever imagined and create something remarkable. Never forget that they are your allies as you head into the metaphorical battle against Vision Killers.

In the previous section, you and your team identified potential objections before spreading the word about the Vision. Now you want to collaborate on creating a road map of *where* to search for potential people to share your Vision and uncover solutions to those challenges. Note: You still aren't trying to solve them. Not yet. You are establishing conviction by pointing everyone in the direction, which lends further credence to the notion that the Vision is attainable.

Allow me to provide a simple example. Suppose you've created the following Vision: *Create a new and unique Internet—one that contains the same information and may be searched with ease but is based on a new process borrowed from blockchain technology that will revolutionize the accuracy of data search results.* There are myriad execution issues involved in this fictional example, so how do we begin to tackle it?

Let's pose a question: *How will the technology work to provide such accurate data search results?*

The Vision Maker team is aware they don't have the answer to this question…yet. But they know several sources where they may discover the answer. For example, it may not be widely known that their parent company just acquired a small tech company that happens to have expertise in this strategic area of blockchain. By conveying this piece of information with the objection, your conviction will have been strengthened because you have an important point of reference.

It may or may not be the ultimate solution, but it conveys a confident temperament right out of the starting gate.

The Leader Must Be Fully Engaged in the Sharing Process

All too often, I've seen the leader complete work with the Vision Maker team, clap her or his hands, proudly declare "We did it!" and then become disassociated from the Vision-sharing process. Relying upon a series of appointed ambassadors, the leader recedes into the background and moves on to other business. Whether the leader is shy or feels under- or overqualified to participate in this process is irrelevant. A negative perception of her or his temperament at this stage can make or break wide acceptance of the Vision.

Here is what the organization might be thinking:

1. The leader had nothing to do with the Vision Maker process.
2. The leader lacks conviction in the Vision.
3. The leader is unenthusiastic about the Vision.
4. The leader won't provide the tools and resources necessary to execute on the Vision.
5. The leader isn't going to see the Vision through to the end.
6. The Vision doesn't have a chance of succeeding if the leader isn't part of the rollout because she or he has the essential knowledge needed to explain its rationale.

Additionally, the leader brings in certain intangibles, such as having had more intimate experiences with the Vision than others in the organization. For instance, imagine the following Vision: *We are going to feed the world.* In this example, the leader might have started out years earlier by establishing a charity for feeding the needy in her or his hometown. This leader has gravitas and can take the opportunity to share the Vision through storytelling (for example, describing a case from her hometown in which a homeless boy's life was saved by the community's efforts).

Another pitfall I've seen is when the leader has a magnificent Vision but gets bogged down discussing execution details during the presentation. The individuals in the organization who are adept at execution take this as a cue to jump in and criticize the leader and the Vision. Additionally, the steps involved in execution tend to be the most boring and least inspirational aspects of the Vision. You want your stakeholders to be pumped about the Vision, not whisked away to dreamland or drowning in execution issues.

The Vision requires respect and TLC. If you are the organization's leader, don't delegate communication to other people. You may assign certain aspects of the presentation to members of Vision Maker team, but you must be front and center to demonstrate complete engagement and support, which can be contagious and help spread excitement through the ranks.

The same goes for various checkpoints throughout the year. In the subsequent months, when addressing the organization at company meetings, leadership reminders of the Vision and the company's progress toward achieving it are essential to keep the momentum going.

Sharing Your Work on Temperament with Ambassadors

The story of Vision sharing is one of collaboration. The phrase "If it is to be, it is up to me" is being replaced because it's inefficient in today's environment. It's no longer about you or even the Vision Maker team. Instead, you must now focus on the enrollment of ambassadors in collaboration.

Your Vision Maker team is already enrolled because its members helped create the Vision in the first place. An ambassador hasn't been part of the process, invested the time and effort, or faced objections. You need to ensure that your ambassadors are enthusiastic, prepared, and know how to deal with potential objections.

First, provide them with materials about the Vision. They may be in the form of written Word documents, PDFs, slide shows, ads, or videos. Any communication may be helpful if it's easily shared.

Consider the Vision of Dove, the company that produces soap: "We believe beauty should be a source of confidence, and not anxiety." If you were to provide the organization's ambassadors with the ability to support this Vision, you might introduce a series of commercials. The Dove organization has already done just that. Their heartfelt commercials—which may be found with a quick Google search—are easily shared. Their ambassadors not only use the product, they also want to feel confident, not anxious. This series of commercials arms the ambassadors against the common objection: "Aren't all soaps the same?" Their answer would be a resounding *No*.

When you announce your Vision to the world, make sure you reach your team, your ambassadors, your clients, your customers (including future ones), your friends, and everyone else you encounter. Imagine what happens when your ambassadors repeat the same messaging simultaneously: The Vision gains even more momentum. The results can be breathtaking.

In the meantime, you need to learn how to overcome initial objections, which we cover in depth in the next chapter.

Chapter Eight

Overcoming Initial Objections

Mark my words: For all your team's brilliant Vision-Making efforts during these first few weeks, you are still likely going to be hammered by objections from all sides. Some left-brain individuals who want proof supported by data will likely question the logic and validity behind the Vision and fire shots at it. The "doers" involved in processes will pose challenging questions, doubting the organization's ability to execute on the Vision; some going as far as saying, "It's impossible" and "It'll never happen." These naysayers believe what they are saying with heart and soul; they can't help venting their true feelings, as they don't want to disappoint leadership by not delivering on expectations or see the company fail.

The other group, mentioned in earlier chapters, are those who want to obliterate the Vision just for the sake of it. Whether they are unhappy in general, bear a grudge, feel left out, are averse to change, or are soured by the company itself, these individuals will do anything within their power to derail efforts. It's possible they might state their objections outright, but more likely, they will do so in passive-aggressive fashion behind the scenes. They will attempt to contaminate others in the organization by poisoning the Vision with concerns that may be real or fabricated, simply to grow the opposition numbers and force abandonment of the whole thing. Some of this behavior may be to get a few kicks and cause confusion, but mainly it's to be "right" and place a dark cloud over the initiative.

The Vision Makers must always stand tall, strong, and united. It's time for you to be proud of the group's efforts and the result. You've come this far in the process, which means that none of the negative efforts could or should hold you back from spreading the message. As we've emphasized throughout, your Vision is bigger than you and must be defended and protected at all costs, even when you recognize the legitimate objections that will be strategically tackled at the right time.

Over the course of several years working as a Vision Maker coach, I've seen and heard it all when it comes to raised objections. I boiled them down to the top twenty, categorizing them by general themes for easier assimilation. This is by no means a complete list of objections, as it would be an impossible endeavor to identify them all. I'm sure you will encounter at least a couple of doozies not specifically listed here as you spread the message of your Vision. The intent is that the responses I provide will arm you with enough ammunition to tailor your remarks as needed.

Who Cares?

Objection Number One

I wasn't invited to serve on the Vision Maker team, so why should I care?

Prior to sharing the Vision—and well before this question can surface—it's a good idea to convey the rich story of how the Vision originated and then took shape as a small group collaborative process. If the person was not included by intent, be authentic, as she or he will pick up on it right away. Part of good Vision leadership is being a leader and accepting your decisions. You might explain that you sought a reasonably sized group consisting of diverse members who fit the criteria with representative Avatars.

If you intended to exclude them because of their focus on *how*, explain that they are valued for picking apart ideas. Back then, you needed to first play out the idea fully without restrictions, but now is the time when they can get involved and shine.

If you had to exclude people because you had too many candidates, then make it clear that it isn't possible to include everyone in the beginning stages. However, this person is now being consulted and will be instrumental in engaging the entire organization moving forward and addressing any objections and concerns. It is extremely important that you acknowledge her or his feelings, rather than just explain your decision. It is effective to simply listen and ask the participant to voice any objections in greater detail. The simple question "Tell me more about that" can solicit their true intentions, thoughts, and misgivings. When the individual is done, repeat back what was said. When the person feels heard and acknowledged, she or he is more likely to listen to your reasoning, rather than continue to object or begrudge your decisions.

If the objection persists in a public forum, it probably means the individual is already soured on the initiative due to exclusion or some other underlying issue specific to that person, such as disgruntlement. Rather than steer the conversation away from the subject at hand and drain company time, it's best to nip this in the bud by saying, "We hear you. You make a good point." Remind the objector that, while you want to forge a great Vision by raising valid objections, the focus must be on how to *overcome* them, not defeat the Vision itself. Conclude by suggesting: "Let's discuss this in greater detail offline, so we may move on with our agenda, as we have limited time and want to hear from everyone. Thank you."

After the meeting is over and the smoke has cleared, set up the meeting with the person who raised the objection of being left out. During the session, make it clear that you appreciate her or his thoughts and respect the point of view raised. Reemphasize that a difficult leadership decision on inclusion had to be made, but that is in the past, and the important focus is now on the challenges that lie ahead. Give the individual an opportunity to tell you how the Vision might be different if she or he had participated in the proceedings. Chances are, there is nothing specific; the colleague will, hopefully, begin assimilating thoughts on how to move forward.

If, however, the colleague continues to seem rankled even after a reasonable period, stand behind the Vision Maker team and the creation. State the following words: "I'm sorry you feel this way. But there will be other opportunities and ways for you to contribute down the road." Then pose the question: "Will you agree to bring up your concerns in a positive way and help us to make this Vision a reality?" Remind the objector of a key principle throughout this book: "A Vision is rarely wrong. We simply have objections on how to implement it." Next, ask: "At the moment, I understand how you feel that the Vision is elusive. Putting all that aside, if your concerns were magically resolved right now, do you think the Vision is a good one?"

By this point, you have put in a great deal of time and effort to explain the rationale behind how the Vision Maker team was created. If the objector still can't get on board with the initiative, you may need to think about how she or he negatively impacts other personnel and reconsider this person's role in the organization.

Objection Number Two
I don't get why this is important.

Apathetic reactions are perhaps even more difficult to deal with than negative resistance. When you are presenting the Vision in a room full of people, you can expect to find several cheerleaders, a few verbal antagonists, a bunch who are on the fence, and a handful who just don't understand the point and think it's a complete waste of time. The telltale signs of the last group will be obvious: they are scrolling on their phones with their necks craned down; folding their arms; buttoning their lips; elbowing people beside them to say, "Listen to this nonsense"; or probably not doing much to hide their snide or bored expressions.

There is nothing worse for a leader than presenting a Vision to someone who doesn't get the Vision or even see the need to have one. This can feel like a stand-up comedian who has exceptionally funny material but can't win over the hecklers and uninitiated in the audience.

Be prepared to overcome this objection. Consider several impactful stories about companies that I highlighted in this book or those of large, successful organizations such as below that have had breakout Visions. On the surface, they may seem like grandiose examples compared to your organization, but they aren't when you consider how far these businesses rose from the ashes. No matter where your company is currently positioned, it couldn't be worse than the low points experienced by these businesses, which were laughingstocks at one time or another:

- **Apple's Vision:** *To make the best products on earth and to leave the world better than we found it.*
  In 1997, Apple faced certain bankruptcy with massive declines in each of the previous dozen years. That year, when Steve Jobs reentered the picture with a refreshed Vision, the company's turnaround and comeback was almost immediate; it went on to become the innovative juggernaut it is today, now valued at over $2.3 trillion.

- **Airbnb's Vision:** *Belong anywhere.*
  Back in 2008, Airbnb didn't seem to belong anywhere. No one wanted to invest in it. As a last resort, the company founders had to create custom cereal boxes to raise funds for a startup incubator and stay afloat. The Vision caught on and its current estimated net worth stands at $78.64 billion.

- **Netflix's Vision:** *Entertain the world.*
  Netflix had been a rollercoaster business for many years after its founding in 1997. Originally, the business concept was to knock out DVD/video retailers by curbing late fees on rentals. The company faced numerous crises until 2013 when it made a pivotal move: creating Netflix original films and TV series and leveraging its subscriber base to increase viewership. Looking back, the idea of "entertaining the world" may seem comically delusional, but they have had the last laugh with a current net worth of over $141.24 billion.

The above examples prove beyond a shadow of a doubt that you can't make it big without *thinking big*. Recount these stories and consider talking about the story the old man shares with Kat at the beginning of this section involving the Pitaya fruit and how the Mariachi festival spread the Vision message, against all odds sustaining the future of the town of Ejutla. Emphasize the following: "If that struggling community can achieve something bigger than they are, so can we!"

Consider handing your people a copy of this book or sections to read and encourage a conversation about the content. This will get them thinking like you. Remember: You are creating a new and different way to think, and your enlightenment may need to be shared with them, so that they have the insight to think differently.

When you are done presenting this counter-objection, you will likely be able to do a mic drop to a standing ovation!

Huh?

The second objection raised after "Who cares?" is almost always "Huh?" which can be translated along the lines of "I don't get it." Try as you might, some people simply might not understand the Vision, relate to it, or follow how it impacts them. We'll put aside those who "play dumb" out of some form of passive-aggressiveness and/or hostility and concentrate on the folks who are truly confused or lost. I don't mean to in any way imply that these people are "slow on the uptake." There are sometimes good, smart people who just aren't tracking with the logic or passion of the Vision-Making team. Sometimes it takes repeated explanations from multiple people to enable them to process the Vision, internalize it, and catch up. Try to be as patient as you can with them.

Recognize the fact that people process things differently. There is a great deal of excellent published literature—for example, *Getting to Yes*, *The 5 Love Languages*, and *How to Win Friends and Influence People*—involving the art of persuasion and how to enroll others to your thoughts, especially according to personality type or brain wiring. An analytical person, for example, rarely speaks in terms of passion or feelings. Someone who processes new ideas via auditory skills versus the written word may have difficulty getting the Vision from a sheet of paper, preferring to hear what it's all about.

People receive messages through their personal "love languages" —a set of rules that allows them to absorb information according to their preferred communication platform. NLP, Neuro-Linguistic Programming, offers several lessons in effective communication through representation constructs. This book isn't designed to summarize or outline these options, but you would be well served by considering the audience you are presenting to and attempting to connect with their method of receiving new ideas. One size doesn't fit all. More likely than not, the issue is one of communicating effectively, rather than the inability of a team member to understand the Vision.

Objection Number Three
I don't understand it—and I hear other people saying the same thing.

In these circumstances, it's helpful to first find out what, specifically, the objectors don't understand. If enough people believe the Vision lacks clarity, it's possible that the statement itself may require further wordsmithing. Chances are this isn't the case, however, and you will need to take some time to unpack what the Vision statement means in more concrete terms. Sometimes projecting what the Vision looks like down the road in its idyllic form can be beneficial to people who don't understand it.

Storytelling is enormously impactful—especially if the Vision has roots stemming from the founder's original concept of the company years earlier. For example, in the case of a healthcare company with a Vision along the lines of "We will provide an unparalleled experience as the most trusted partner for healthcare," the founder might discuss having been a sickly child who survived life-threatening pneumonia or the fear associated with not having a reliable partner to guide the family through the illness. The excellent care she received not only saved her life, but it also planted the seed for her later dream of helping others.

Also consider telling a future tale, one people can relate to that is laced with examples of how this Vision will favorably impact the world in a concrete way. You may already have one such emotionally powerful story that is part of the fabric of your company's history and in some way inspired the Vision itself.

You Don't Know Anything

Objection Number Four
You don't have it right.

This can be challenging to navigate, especially in technology-related companies where the engineers are perfectionists and often have a firmer grasp on the technical aspects of what the company does every day. It's okay to concede this point. Acknowledge that you respect their talents and skills and don't pretend to be at their level of sophisticated understanding and capability. Being humble can go a long way toward earning trust.

At the same time, keep in mind that, while workers are being paid for their knowledge and training, it doesn't mean that they have your ability to see past the tasks that are directly in front of them. You, as the leader, are there for that purpose: You are looking into the future and what the company can ultimately become in its best form. Think of it this way: Did Steve Jobs physically build the iPhone? Of course not. He had an army of people who could accomplish that for the company. However, he did have a Vision that was bigger than Apple at the time and was able to see all the possibilities that lay ahead leading to the creation of the iPhone. Similarly, Amazon—whose Vision is "...to be earth's most customer-centric company; to build a place where people can come to find and discover anything they might want to buy online"—is an excellent example of a technology-based company that is focused on Vision, not the other way around.

You know much more than you think. At the same time, you also admire and respect what the team members bring to the table. Emphasize how much you trust them to take the ball and run with it and make the Vision a reality. Challenge their thinking to focus on ways to overcome the *how*. Remind them that there have been countless historical stories of seemingly impossible situations that were overcome through human ingenuity and tenacity. The 1970 Apollo 13 mission was one such example, in which American astronauts were stuck in a capsule in space with insufficient power and oxygen to return safely to Earth. The Vision of returning was clear, but the *how* seemed impossible. It would have been easy for them to have thrown in the towel and conceded to failure, but instead they were inspired to think creatively and problem-solve with the instruments and tools available.

You don't need to be in a crisis to overcome obstacles in achieving your Vision. You merely need to believe in it and everyone's ability to collaborate and serve as a single-minded unit to figure out the *how*.

Objection Number Five
I am the expert, not you.

This is like Objection Four, except the objector is taking the position of having intellectual superiority and challenging the Vision based on that knowledge. Don't act defensive or try to prove that you know more than the person. In fact, the best course is to do the exact opposite by acknowledging that she or he is essential to developing the *how*. After all, you hired this individual for those precise skills in the first place.

Continue to press the team member to acknowledge the Vision and consider whether it *could* be done. Overcome their distrust of your ability by providing famous examples of Visions that weren't considered "good enough." Experts make mistakes all the time. A physician named Dr. Raymond V. Damadian once had a Vision that it would be possible to take a picture of inside the human body without usage of any radiation (i.e., an x-ray). He was ridiculed, scorned, and denied funds for a research study. People dismissed his Vision as being "impossible" and "impractical." In 1977, against all odds, Dr. Damadian successfully performed the first official MRI (magnetic resonance imaging), which revolutionized modern science. Not only could one view inside the human body without radiation, but it also suddenly became possible to see soft tissue that hadn't been visible with a traditional x-ray, making it a superior diagnostic tool to reveal many diseases and conditions.

Here are three more examples of when certain "experts" had it wrong about major talents:

- The Beatles—who became the world's greatest rock band—famously failed their audition for Decca Records on January 1, 1962. Their music executive, Dick Rowe, told Brian Epstein, the group's manager: "Guitar groups are on their way out." Boy was he on the wrong side of history!

- Filmmaker extraordinaire Steven Spielberg was rejected by the University of Southern California School of Theatre, Film and Television no less than *three times.*

- Stephen King's classic novel *Carrie* was rejected by *thirty publishers.* One editor commented: "We are not interested in science fiction which deals with negative utopias. They do not sell." The book was indeed published, in 1974, and has reportedly sold over four million copies since (and has twice been adapted into films).

- George Michael's famous song "Careless Whisper" was rejected as being out of sync when it was written. Most didn't even know it was one of his first written songs until a recent documentary on the group Wham!

It's All Big Talk—Nothing Ever Sticks

As we know, Visions often stop and start and come and go. Some workers have been through several cycles of Vision creation that failed to gain traction, so you can understand why they might be skeptical about this one standing the test of time. Let's look at the two common objections that fall under this general umbrella.

Objection Number Six
You are going to change your mind about the Vision in three months and rewrite it, so why bother?

You'll want to put yourself in the shoes of people who have spent a lot of time developing—or cheerleading—Vision statements in the past that were scrapped and overhauled. It can be quite frustrating for workers to have chased after the soccer ball back and forth so many times. Acknowledge their feelings right away; transparency always helps earn trust.

Depending on your situation, you can admit that past Vision initiatives didn't have things quite right because they weren't *big enough*. If you're a Visionary who has proposed other Visions but then went on to another shiny object, inform the objector why this endeavor is different. On this occasion, you have discussed your Vision with a team, vetted it, and devoted a great deal of time and effort into enrolling others to make it come true. This is far different than the previous ideas you had that were couched in Vision. You are exercising the ability to be a Vision Maker—not an idea person or a Visionary— which is a distinction we made in earlier chapters. This Vision will sing because it has champions—including those who were skeptics at first—who will help announce it to the world. Demonstrate your work, thoughts, and process that brought you to this current state of having a true Vision with substance.

Objection Number Seven
You are going to forget about it in a month, so why bother?

This is where you must demonstrate your commitment to the Vision. Establish a schedule of discussions that includes specific key performance indicators you expect your team to develop with firm dates. Then it becomes up to you to set up regular days/times for check-ins. The type of person who raises Objection Seven is sure to test how serious you are about the time frame, so it's crucial for team members to deliver on expectations.

You will probably encounter those who couldn't find or make the time to complete the action items that were due for completion by the first and second meetings. This is when strong leadership comes in. If you don't hold people accountable early on, none of the deadlines will be met by anyone on the team because the effort doesn't seem to be taken seriously enough. This only reinforces the objector's issue that the initiative "will be forgotten about in a month," which you can't allow to happen.

Gently remind all team members that they must be committed to the Vision and that you expect all steps to be carried out by the agreed upon deadlines. Imply that the Vision lives with them, but if they are unwilling to see it through, you will have to seek others who will do so. Be subtle, not threatening, as it will show resolve.

Another idea to keep things on track is to split your team into two equal sides. Create a friendly competition between them to see who can produce the fastest (or most effective) results on the action list. You can even give out prizes (or a company perk) to the winning team as an incentive. These kinds of engaging activities will motivate people while at the same time encouraging some competitive fun.

To further prove the Vision's longevity, it should be memorialized in the organization wherever possible for maximum exposure. Below are a few starter locations:

- Create a tab for it on the company's website.
- Enable it to appear on the company's intranet, so it becomes the first thing workers see when they log in.
- Include the Vision as part of your email signature.
- Emblazon the Vision on the hallway of the office lobby.
- Based on your budget, consider creating swag featuring the Vision to hand out to everyone for free: water bottles, t-shirts, pins, notebooks, mugs, backpacks, Post-Its, folders, etc.
- At every company meeting, tie in new initiatives to the Vision. Make sure that department heads and supervisors are reinforcing the Vision at team meetings and during their one-on-one sessions with those that report directly to them.

There is no need to feel limited to just these ideas. Solicit suggestions from the team to come up with ways to send positive reminders to everyone about the Vision. You will be amazed by the wealth of creativity that heads your way!

Change Is Scary

George Bernard Shaw once said, "Progress is impossible without change, and those who cannot change their minds cannot change anything."

Most people loathe change, unless they are the ones who proposed it in the first place. Even the most beneficial changes in an organization can cause resentment among the ranks. You'll often hear individuals push back with statements such as: "Why do we have to change things? Everything is working just fine!"

A grand Vision *should* change the status quo in an organization and coax everyone into thinking differently. They may ultimately come around to being thrilled about the idea behind the Vision, but still have genuine concerns on a personal level that you will need to address.

Zapping the Vision Killers

If fear seems to be an overriding emotion in your group, initiate an activity I call "Fear Therapy." Have everyone write down something that "scares" or "concerns" them about the Vision. The participants should fold up their papers and place them in a bag or hat. Individuals then pluck out a random piece of folded paper from the receptacle. Each person reads the fear aloud, one by one, and then presents a reason why no one should fear it (or a way to diffuse it). If the speaker receives the fear that she or he wrote, that's perfectly fine—that person still needs to counter it (or the group can help). If multiple people are afraid of the same thing, the counterargument must be different each time (which leads to a range of potential solutions). This activity serves several purposes, including enabling people to empathize with each other and realize they are not the only ones who are afraid. Another upside is that a wealth of antifear ammunition will be spread throughout the room, which curbs the need for anyone to express the same concern again.

Objection Number Eight

We are already doing several things that fall outside this Vision—are we going to cancel them?

An organization must focus on doing what it does best and the things that help grow the Vision—the *flywheels*, to coin the usage from Jim Collins's *Good to Great*. The reality is that, while other unrelated parts of the company may employ people who served a purpose at one time or another, they probably don't feed the bottom line or contribute to the future. This can lead to some tricky situations for the leader, who may not yet be prepared to make decisions about folding certain parts of the business—and that is okay. Assure everyone that what is being done does not necessarily stop while you are creating a Vision for the future. If it does seem likely that some phases of business will be dropped, there are myriad ways to transition individuals into newer and better roles that are conducive to fulfilling the Vision.

For the most part, fears of becoming obsolete are unfounded. Years ago, the thought of robots building cars was greatly opposed by assembly line workers, but look at the state of things today: Who programs and maintains the robots, makes sure they are performing to expectations, and recommends changes? The employees who know how to assemble the cars, of course.

Objection Number Nine

Are people going to lose their jobs?

The answer at this stage is an emphatic "No." To reiterate the messaging from the last objection, the Vision is only about mapping the future and not job cuts.

If this objection arises, assure everyone that you are only focused on the Vision at this present time, and there are no plans to let anyone go. Expansion of the Vision often leads to even greater opportunity for workers.

Encourage people to become interested in the Vision and immerse themselves in it as the strategy unfolds. Try to get the point across that the future is filled with opportunities and will open the doors for the evolution of more exciting roles and types of work. You are looking for everyone to be curious and creative while discovering how the Vision will shape the company.

We Have More Important Things to Do Right Now

You are also likely to encounter objections from those who can't see the forest for the trees. It's not necessarily that they don't care about the company or even what it stands for; they simply don't see it as a priority when there are so many other things to do. These individuals may assert that a Vision is a nice thing to have when there is time, but it's a "soft initiative" compared to things such as meeting revenue goals.

Alternatively, they might espouse something along the lines of, "Why are we doing this? We already know who we are and what we do. Why are you preaching the obvious to us? Why can't we just do our jobs?"

These are reasonable things to ask, but they must be diffused right away. Let's break these down into the next two related but separate objections.

Objection Number Ten
This is an unnecessary waste of time.

Believe or not, I've worked with CEOs, CFOs, and other company executives who have uttered statements such as the above. In case you haven't heard my message by now, I'll reiterate it one more time: *Nothing* is more important to an organization than the Vision. Without it, there *is* no future!

In addition to this response—which may come across as a bit too broad—you need to outline for people the underlying purposes of the Vision, which may be tailored to suit your organization's situation. For example, the Vision might be used as a recruiting and onboarding tool by human resources and hiring managers—something that has become more of a challenge when there is a limited candidate pool and young workers want to serve organizations that offer more than just a paycheck. It may also be a great source for identifying new product lines and services for customers, which will lead to increased revenue and profit. Marketing and sales professionals should also appreciate the fact that the Vision will better communicate, to partners, vendors, and consumers who—like employees—want to know and better understand the people they are working with, as well as the purpose of their purchases. When your Vision is bigger than you, others want to jump on board and the entire organization experiences a fission-type chain reaction that propels success. These are the focus points that make Vision too important to ignore or put on a back burner.

Objection Number Eleven
I don't have time for this.

It can be said that *time* is the biggest Vision Killer of them all. However, this is a mindset issue, not a reality. Ask the objector (or yourself, if it's you): "What is more important—the tasks of the day or a Vision that is bigger than we are and, therefore, should be brought out into the world? You want to make an impact, right? Here is your chance to do it!"

We are all strapped for time, juggling a million different things every day. Even the busiest individuals can carve out a small amount of time devote to the Vision. If you have concerns, consider scheduling a standing appointment—at least a half an hour—on your calendar every day to spread the message of the Vision and strategize the rollout. If you or anyone else continues to express that there isn't enough available time, test the theory out. For three days straight, write down everything you did at work and at home in ten-minute increments. When you see what's on the list, you will identify several idle things that could be repurposed or dropped entirely. Rarely have I ever found an executive or employee who couldn't devote enough time to an important project like this.

I once had an experience at a weeklong men's leadership retreat that changed my relationship with time and my attitude toward it. For one of the solo exercises, I was assigned to design a shelter to house future teams from inclement weather. I was provided the necessary materials and a time limit—but nothing else. I spent the day working feverishly on the project. I was almost done when a leader appeared in a golf cart, summoning me to attend an urgent meeting a mile and a half away. He drove off without me. I had to abandon my project and jog to the meeting place.

I was irritated, to say the least. I muttered to myself during my entire trip to join the meeting. "How can they do this? Why would they interrupt me—don't they realize I'm trying to get this project done? I'm not finished. I had at least another hour left, according to the schedule… This isn't leadership, it's *slave labor!*"

When I arrived, I couldn't believe what I saw. Forty others in the program were showing up at the same time, half out of breath from jogging there and muttering to themselves—just as I had been doing. A few minutes later, the program leader addressed the confused crowd: "Take a moment to absorb what you are feeling. Identify it, hold onto it, and amplify it for one minute."

Sixty seconds passed when suddenly, off to our right, the doors of a barnlike structure opened. Large round rubber balls were released into the crowd. Hoses were turned on. Water balloons were carried out in a wagon. We were told to choose sides for a water fight.

All forty of us charged in and engaged in battle. We had a blast running around soaking each other and couldn't stop laughing. When the balloons were all spent, the water spigots turned off. We continued to laugh and joke around as we gathered. We still wondered what that was all about but, truthfully, no longer cared all that much because we'd had so much fun.

"How do you feel now?" the leader asked the group.

Aha! My anger and frustration had dissipated. More to the point, I had forgotten all about completing my project. Later, we were granted permission to resume work on our respective projects. We did so willingly and in good spirits. We even helped each other out.

We learned something invaluable from this experience: *Time is what you make of it.* We all have time, but sometimes we convince ourselves that not enough is available to us. How we choose to spend our time is exactly that: *a choice.*

Objection Number Twelve

The economy is spiraling. How can we even think about a Vision when the worst might happen? We need to spend our time preparing...

When it comes to the economy, there is only one thing we know for sure: It can spiral *anytime* for *any* reason. Who could have predicted events such as 9/11, the COVID-19 shutdowns, radical inflation hikes, Russia's invasion of Ukraine, and how each of these events ended up having an impact on so many things?

Life is too short, and we can't go around worried that the sky is always about to fall. That will never lead to business growth or create the path to achieve your Vision. Yes, we want to safeguard our businesses and be prepared to do what's right for all kinds of situations. To paraphrase nineteenth-century UK Prime Minister Benjamin Disraeli: "Be prepared for the worst, hope for the best."

While it's potentially true that a recession could wreak havoc on your business, consider the fact that *not* having a Vision in place could lead to the same result. The good news is that the economy is cyclical, and nothing stays the same for long. The same may be said for a powerful Vision which, hopefully, is so magnificent it can withstand any type of financial crisis. The current buzz word is *pivot*, which anyone can do. At the height of the COVID-19 pandemic, so many business leaders found ways to pivot that it was almost magical; they profited, despite all the gloom and doom. It's all about asking, "How can I do this differently?"

Objection Number Thirteen

If we share the Vision before we've secured marketplace dominance, someone will steal it.

This is another objection related to time: Is there such a thing as sharing a Vision *too soon*?

If the Vision is ready for prime time, it's not too soon to unveil it to the world. You don't need to be afraid that someone will steal it. Mainly, you should be viewing your Vision as authentic to you and your organization. Your competitor's version will pale in comparison to yours and won't sustain itself because it wasn't created with the same blood, sweat, and tears. Additionally, their Vision will face severe public scrutiny when it's exposed as not being the brand's unique, original identity. Today's younger generations place great value on strong ethics, so be confident that you are standing on the high ground, and you will always win in the end.

Here's Why It Won't Work

I saved the biggest grouping of objections for last: The argument that the Vision is doomed to failure. It's way too easy to come up with all kinds of reasons why something will tank and make that the excuse in advance for why it didn't work. Some people enjoy feeling high and mighty at the prospect of later saying, "See, I told you so!"

As I stated earlier, the organization could be headed to the brink on its *current* trajectory. There are no guarantees of anything, but often plodding along the same course without a Vision—a True North—will only risk causing the ship to get lost and/or strike an iceberg. Consider the path of a tree, for example. It must continue to grow, or it will die. There isn't such a thing as status quo because at some point natural calamities occur that knock down old branches; without new ones sprouting out, the tree will wither. The same is true for businesses.

I know of a Conservative Jewish synagogue on the East Coast that has had dwindling membership every year for the past five years. The reasons for this are easy to follow: there are fewer Conservative Jewish people in the area (and in general); the new families that are moving in feel less of an obligation to join a synagogue than prior generations; and they just don't believe they can spare the money for dues with the cost of living and inflation being so high. The finance committee estimated that, at the current pace, the synagogue would be bankrupt in perhaps three years—five tops. The leadership team then discovered that a neighboring Conservative Jewish congregation was already teetering on the edge of bankruptcy and had a building on the verge of collapse. So, discussions took place between the two respective leadership teams to consolidate and form one substantial, magnificent synagogue.

Most synagogue members understood the situation and the benefits of a merger, especially since it would rescue both entities from their financial challenges. But there were a few congregants at the first synagogue who said, "Eh, we'll be fine—we don't need them. Who knows what'll happen in three or five years. Maybe membership will go up again!"

While it's always possible for miracles to happen, it's more important to read the writing on the wall and understand where your organization stands from a variety of viewpoints (especially financial). By doing nothing in the case of the synagogue merger, it's certain that at some point *both* congregations will eventually fold. Why not save them both by consolidating and creating a unique new Vision?

Many people believe that sharks die if they don't keep moving. That's not exactly true. Sharks need to keep moving or else they risk sinking to the bottom of the water column. Consider this metaphor for your organization: If you don't keep moving, you will sink to the bottom.

Objection Number Fourteen
We don't have enough of a workforce to fulfill the Vision.

The cliché "the cart before the horse" comes to mind with this objection. First comes the Vision-Making process, followed by the rollout, the strategy, and then the execution. When someone voices this concern, simply reply, "We don't know yet what workforce we'll need to fulfill the Vision. We'll address resource needs once we've built the strategy. Let's take this one step at a time."

Presenting a rough timeline can also sometimes be useful to help people understand that the Vision initiative will unfold in increments over time. Once you've hit certain benchmarks—including creation and approval of a budget with a line item for resources—you'll solve the workforce issues.

Objection Number Fifteen
We're having enough trouble just filling open positions. We will never be able to recruit the talent and skill sets needed to fulfill the Vision.

The answer to Objection Fourteen applies here as well, with one additional upside: The Vision is so appealing and grand that it will help recruit fresh talent to fill open positions and new ones that may arise as the Vision unfurls. The Vision is a recruitment tool for human resources and hiring managers, demonstrating to candidates that the company has specific direction and a bright future.

Objection Number Sixteen

We've already explored this Vision years ago and it failed. Why will it work now?

The way to counter this objection is by admitting to prior setbacks and emphasizing how much you've learned since then. You are far more educated now than years earlier and have had the benefit of the Vision Maker team to iron out the kinks. You are also supporting the Vision in a way that it hadn't been in the past. Previous efforts most likely failed due to premature evaluations by the Vision Killers, not the Vision itself.

Objection Number Seventeen

Others have attempted this Vision and failed.

This is a variant of Objection Sixteen. As a leader, you are well within your right to pump up your chest and respond with the exclamation: "*They are not us!*"

Do not worry about your competition when it comes to Vision. If they failed at something similar, it's likely because they didn't have such an amazing Vision Maker team and an organization like yours that is well versed in the process. Your competitor probably gave up way too soon on their Vision, something that your solid company will not do.

Objection Number Eighteen

We don't have the funds to support such a Vision.

This is probably why you need a spectacular Vision in the first place: It will help you spread the word of the Vision, which in turn will facilitate soliciting funds as needed. Friends, family, angel investors, or venture capital investors might be welcome, but that isn't necessarily the direction you need to head toward. There are many options you can cite, namely crowdfunding, grants, SBA loans, and more. Either way, firmly tell your objectors that the funds will be there once the Vision is announced and gains momentum. People love to join causes, such as a powerful, meaningful Vision. Take a cue from Kat's original effort with the mountain climb described in the introduction to Week II. She didn't fall short of her fundraising effort because of a poor Vision; she simply didn't broadcast it well enough to the world.

Objection Number Nineteen
We do not know the right people that can get your Vision off the ground.
I love the phrase "If you build it, they will come" in the film *A Field of Dreams*. In this case, we are of course talking about a Vision that is bigger than you—not summoning the ghosts of the 1919 Chicago Black Sox baseball team. State loud and clear to the objector that you *will* know the right people through appropriate outreach channels. I've witnessed people successfully solicit other CEOs to become involved. Outreach efforts might involve social media posts, meetup groups, chamber groups, and other local or national organizations. LinkedIn is an exceptional place to search for businesses, organizations, and specific individuals who might be interested in the Vision and provide the targeted support you need.

Objection Number Twenty
We do not know the technology to make the Vision come true.
Once the strategy is in place and you have knowledgeable people aboard and sustainable funding, the technology will materialize. This might happen through internal innovation and/or recruitment, but it might also be worthwhile to approach outside partners or outsourced vendors with the right technological DNA. Better yet, you might be able to acquire a small company that brings this technology ready-made to you.

There is no substitute for being able to creatively devise your own solution. As the saying goes, "Necessity is the mother of invention."

I never thought it would be possible, but I once accomplished this myself. Years ago, my clients often asked me to create legal documents for them. I would pay for them to be professionally bound by a printer, but this wasn't always feasible; if a page needed to be changed or altered, it became a major hassle. I conceived a product—a method of securing a stack of paper that was convenient, looked great, and could be done instantly in the office without machinery. More importantly, it could easily be undone to remove, add, and/or replace pages.

Now, I knew absolutely nothing about plastics, binding documents, or molds to manufacture such a device. However, when I asked around, I was introduced to a plastics engineer. We hit it off and became partners. He created at least ten iterations of this device until we got it just right. The product became a reality and solved my problem. I even managed to patent it.

Ironically, at the time I didn't yet have the understanding contained in this book and didn't create a Vision for the product. I didn't have a clue how to spread the word about the binding technique and never brought it to market.

Please—don't make my mistake! Always follow your gut, create a Vision beyond your wildest imagination, and take whatever steps are necessary to get it done. Any objections?

Chapter Nine

Converting Apathy to Advocacy

Who cares? How does this affect me? Why is this my problem? What's in it for me? Can't you see I have more important things to do? Why are we spending precious time and resources on this?

Question: What do all the above questions have in common?

Answer: They are all apathetic phrases.

Before we delve into combating apathy, we must first define it and place the word in its proper context. The word itself means "general disinterest" or "a lack of concern." When you are apathetic about something, you don't care to be involved or have any skin in the game regarding its outcome one way or the other.

One friend I spoke to about the subject of apathy remarked, "If you don't follow a plan for your life, you are going to fit into someone else's plan." Everyone needs some type of guiding force in life and business, and apathy is not the answer. If you don't have a Vision of your own, that's okay. You can gain a great deal by following the plan of others and, in so doing, reveal your own unique Vision down the road.

Apathy Doesn't Serve You or Others

There is nothing inherently wrong with apathy; it's a normal human emotion, and you can't force someone to feel a certain way. If, for example, someone asks you, "Who are you rooting for in the World Series?" and you answer, "Eh. It doesn't matter to me, I'm not a baseball fan," it won't do you a bit of good to charge back with: "Come on, how can you say that? Baseball is America's favorite pastime! And this is the greatest matchup ever! You have to cheer on the Mets, they're always the underdogs!"

In general, apathy is not a reaction you ever want to see, hear, or feel from anyone who is part of your business endeavor. Ideally, you expect everyone to care about the business from the top on down and to work together positively to achieve common goals. We know this is never 100% possible, of course, as there is inevitably *someone* who is disgruntled about *something* and "just going through the motions." Sometimes this is a result of individual burnout more than the fault of any one leader. Whatever the cause, the result is that leaders tend to motivate the majority and write off the apathetic contingent as a loss. Instead, if you are in this situation with any of your workers, the opposite should occur: You must give it your all to overcome their apathy.

There isn't any room for this emotion when it comes to Vision. Disinterest has the potential to be as damaging—if not more so—than the objections posed in the last chapter. This is true because it can become an even more aggressive contagion and spread rapidly through an organization. If an individual outwardly expresses the apathy to one or more people, it becomes easy for others to verbalize, "Well, if Nikki and Phillippe don't care—why should I?"

Worse yet, apathy can be subtle—possibly even invisible—and yet traces of the feeling will float, spread, and linger in an organization's ecosystem like an infectious microbe infiltrating the human body. Once it's identified as prevalent, it's usually too late to do anything about it—except for one powerful salve.

One of the biggest causes of apathy to spread in an organization is the sentiment that management "doesn't listen" and/or "doesn't care." This may or may not be true, but either way, leadership must immediately address and counter this perception, as it's a sign of a wider cultural issue than just the Vision.

It's impossible to have any chance at bringing hidden apathy out into the light and dealing with it if the population isn't comfortable expressing their views or if there isn't a regular forum for open discussion. In one-on-one, team, and company sessions, leaders must invite people to raise all concerns. Once the issues are expressed, leaders must go out of their way to demonstrate empathy, understanding, and support and avoid being critical or dismissive. One misstep and it's back to rampant statements such as management "doesn't listen" and/or "doesn't care."

If you zap an apathetic culture, you're paving the way for people to be more receptive to hearing and buying into a Vision.

To address this issue, let's study Althea, a woman I met while socializing by a swimming pool. Surrounded by several of her friends—all successful businesspersons—she seemed relaxed as she sipped on a cold beverage. I was friendly with several people in the group, so I joined them and listened to their banter about family, challenges, and their mutual admiration of one another.

A friend turned to me, inquiring about my latest ideas on Vision. I provided them a few details and we had an amiable conversation. When the chitchat touched on business growth and its relationship to Vision, Althea sat up in her chair and snarled, "I'm sorry, I don't care about elephants in Africa. My business has had plenty of success without needing any kind of Vision. Business success is about reality, achieving growth, and profitability."

While I understood she was being sarcastic—we hadn't even hinted about elephants in Africa—her meaning was clear. She didn't have any desire to participate in what she regarded as a meaningless Vision exercise. I could have challenged her but didn't feel it was the appropriate time or place.

Instead, I shared an example of William, a successful business professional who, like her, was a Vision skeptic in the beginning. A successful franchiser of chicken restaurants, William didn't feel he had any time to spend on a discussion pertaining to Vision, but by all measure, he was exceptionally knowledgeable about his industry and skilled at creating thriving establishments without seeming to need one. Despite William's initial resistance, his second-in-command implemented a magnificent Vision—one that attracted myriad investors, suppliers, employees, and franchisees to build the brand even more rapidly than anyone had thought possible. The proud and thankful CEO would later admit that he had become a convert, a true believer in Vision. Althea sat and politely listened. To this day, I remain unsure if she was moved by my example.

Her lack of response didn't faze me a bit. Among all the stories I've shared, this has become my favorite because it forced me to devise a strategy on how to counter blatant apathy about the necessity of a Vision.

Althea seemed to have genuine opposition to such an initiative, which signaled to me that there are many others out there who would display similar apathy. I had to concede that her point had merit and demanded answers to these questions: *Why have a Vision if your business is already flying high? Why should you care enough to put in all that effort?*

No Snap Judgments

A leader's typical emotional response to apathy is anger and defensiveness. You think to yourself: *How dare you question my authority? If I say we need a Vision, we need a Vision!*

If these judgmental feelings are vocalized in any way, the other party will dig even deeper into her apathetic hole. Let's return to the statement made to a person who didn't care about baseball posed earlier in this chapter: "Come on, how can you say that? Baseball is America's favorite pastime! And this is the greatest matchup ever! You have to cheer on the Mets, they're always the underdogs!"

This approach never works. Human beings resist being judged and run in the opposite direction when you force the issue. For example, if I were to have reacted to Althea's anti-Vision stance by saying, "How could you not have a Vision? Every respectable business has a Vision!" she would have been understandably annoyed with me and tuned out everything I might have imparted afterward.

The simple question "How could you not have a Vision?" is already casting judgment. While I believe every organization should have a Vision bigger than themselves, I would never force the issue; not if the leader doesn't want to.

The same is true for nonleaders who work for you and don't care about having a Vision. If you shove it down their throats and criticize them, you'll simply cause more resentment and they'll shut down. Even statements such as "You just don't get it" will be interpreted as off-putting and insulting.

In my opinion, there is no room for judgment when it comes to collaborating with people who are in a different place. Althea doesn't have to care about elephants in Africa. That's her prerogative. Perhaps she'll come around to thinking like a Vision Maker later by witnessing how the process has benefited other organizations. Or maybe her team will demand it of her at some point. In any case, in extreme cases of apathy such as this, the best bet is to keep your judgments to yourself and consider other effective methods of enrollment.

Apathy May Be a Result of Deep-Seated Frustration

One reason to be sympathetic when people react with apathy is that they may have been burned before while getting involved in causes. Who can blame them if they feel they've wasted time and/or money supporting an organization that didn't meet their expectations? From my experience, I'm inclined to believe that apathy is an expression of inward frustration resulting from previous disappointment.

Apathy may also be a defense mechanism. If the leader of a profitable, growing organization tends to be risk averse, a Vision exercise might seem threatening. Since things are going so well, why rock the boat and take a chance of losing what they have? For this reason, they may be less inclined to explore new ideas or hear any challenges to accepted viewpoints. They are living by the cliché "If it ain't broke, don't fix it," which I completely understand.

If you encounter resistance from someone whom you believe is behaving in an apathetic manner for this reason, I suggest that you recommend the individual *explore the idea*. What harm can there be simply joining the team on a journey of discovery? Often the promise of an interesting journey replaces apathy with an opposite emotional response: curiosity or perhaps even anticipation.

If this leader continues to see zero value in the endeavor and shrugs, "Thanks but no thanks. I've been down that road too many times already," try to recruit a recognized expert to work with the person and view the experience through a more polished lens. This route convinced me to participate in a certain activity—hunting geodes, a certain kind of collectible rock form inside holes and crevices of sedimentary rock—after I'd already given up. I had scavenged many mountains on "geode adventures" but never discovered a single rock and found the experiences boring. However, once I tapped an expert for help, I agreed to venture out and try again. I still didn't find anything, but at least this time I knew what I was doing and enjoyed the adventure.

A Healthy Dose of Manifestation

There are some individuals who end up limiting themselves because they fail to recognize the potential in things that don't exist—at least not yet. They need to experience the "finished perfected result" to understand the value of things that are still in the idea stage. This is a prime opportunity for great leaders to step up, as they can inspire others to see what they do.

I have a simple technique to help you fill this role. Start by telling the employee who is expressing apathy to "play in manifestation without any attachment to the outcome." Provide small prompts to help her or him visualize the Vision. If the individual can bear with you—or at least humor you—perhaps she will agree to closing her eyes and picturing it in her mind and then drawing what she thinks the Vision might look like. Involvement in such an exercise might be just enough to engage her further in your initiative.

Introducing: Angel Advocates

We've all heard the phrase "devil's advocate" to refer to someone who has an opposing view on an issue or challenges it to expose potential wrinkles. Sometimes a devil's advocate chooses a stance with good intentions; on other occasions, it's to stir the pot and make things difficult for everyone else. A powerful devil's advocate can dilute, clutter, confuse, delay, and possibly obliterate even the strongest Vision.

On the other end of the spectrum is a type of person we don't hear about often enough: an *angel advocate*. As you've no doubt surmised, this is someone who looks for the positive aspects of a concept and goes out of her or his way to support it. A religious angel advocate involves recruitment of an evangelical nature, but there can be advocates in secular areas, such as politics, as well. No matter the cause, the individual generally shares her views in some type of verbal or written public fashion. The difference between a casual supporter and an angel advocate is that the latter attempts to spread the positive message in the hope of winning people over.

When it comes to your Vision, you want to recruit as many angel advocates as possible to squelch objections and apathy to the point that neither can claim any type of hold on your organization.

Angel Advocates Appear in Many Forms

It goes without saying that the CEO and all other members of the leadership team must be on board with the Vision and fully embrace evangelizing its message both internally and externally. That is the bare minimum—although not nearly enough—for the Vision to spread and grow. Just as you need Vision Makers to create the Vision, you must also have an army of angel advocates to educate people and win over their hearts and minds.

Everyone in your organization has impeccable credentials and enormous skill and/or talent and contributes in some vital way—otherwise, you wouldn't have hired her or him in the first place. Now is the time to look to your entire bench—whether in product development, sales, marketing, customer service, warehousing, fulfillment, or finance/accounting—to devote their respective abilities to the Vision rollout. You want each person at every level to become enlisted and engaged in the process performing at least one specific task—big or small.

Right out of the gate, all angel advocates need a clear path toward achieving measurable success. They must be empowered to propose fresh ideas for spreading the message of the Vision and then take ownership of executing them. Allotting and approving a reasonable spending budget would be wise, as it shows the company is 100% behind the initiative while also preventing spending surprises down the road.

Now that you are sending your gallant angels to march forth and combat apathy and spread the word of your Vision, you are ready to head *beyond* Week III of the process: ensuring that the message is shielded in iron armor, gains momentum, and is built to stand the test of time.

BEYOND WEEK III

How to Sustain the Momentum

THE OLD MAN'S SECRET STRATEGY

Kat was elated to have spent so much time with the old man. He inspired her to develop a plan to advocate for her Vision and start collaborating with a list of people who could help her. Noah was at the top of her list.

Noah, meanwhile, felt even lower than before the trip to Mexico but was reluctant to share his feelings with Kat, as he didn't want to interrupt her enthusiasm. He also remained unclear about what was bothering him.

Three days after returning home, Noah was called into his employer's office. The firm was facing some cutbacks and other belt-tightening measures. While Noah wasn't being let go, he was going to be assigned fewer interesting cases, those typically handed to new and less experienced attorneys.

He arrived home deeply troubled and furious. He guzzled several glasses of wine while waiting for Kat to arrive home from work. She was atypically late and hadn't informed him. He texted her, but she didn't respond.

Privately, he had been seething with jealousy these past couple of weeks. While he was grinding away at his job and now being informed that he was receiving something of a demotion, Kat was enjoying a flurry of success. She was enveloped by new clients and cheerleaders of her Vision.

In that moment, he reflected on something he said to Kat the prior evening that had slipped off his tongue: "I know your company is important, but maybe you can take a break from talking about it so much? All I hear from you is how you're going to 'save the world.'"

Filled with regret, he gulped down the rest of his wine and slumped in the living room chair. A moment later, Kat walked in, bubbly and bright. You'd never know from her energy and aura that she'd put in an eleven-plus-hour workday.

Her upbeat mood reminded him of everything he'd been stewing about. He frowned, refilling his wine glass to the top.

"What's wrong?" she asked.

"Where have you been?" he snapped.

"At work, of course. Where do you think I was?"

"You're late," he assailed her, chugging down more wine. "You didn't let me know or respond to my text."

"You're right," she said, approaching him and stroking her fingers through his hair. This was something he ordinarily liked, but he recoiled from it. "I got caught up with a new client who is in town. You know how it is. I'm so sorry, Noah."

He rose from the chair, storming into the bedroom. Kat thought better of following him, instead deciding to prepare his favorite dinner: Ricotta and Bell Pepper Stuffed Chicken.

Sometime later, when the meal was ready, she called out to Noah—but there was no answer. She went to the bedroom, where she found him on the bed, fast asleep. This wasn't all that surprising to her, as he was a lightweight when it came to alcohol. She pulled the covers over him and turned out the bedroom light before dining by herself in the kitchen. She packed up the rest for Noah to eat whenever he would be ready for it....

■ ■ ■

The next morning, the couple awoke to the confounding bleeping of their alarm clock. Kat reached over to adjust Noah's long hair, which was disheveled and covering his reddened eyes. Clearly, he didn't have a restful sleep, despite his early bedtime.

"Please, tell me...what's wrong, honey?" she asked. "I'm worried."

"I've...been demoted," he croaked, his eyes moistening.

Kat returned his admittance with a grin. Noah misinterpreted this to mean she was mocking him. He sat up and shouted, "I'm serious Kat—they demoted me! I already didn't like a lot of the work they had me do. Now what am I worth? I can't leave. I don't have another job, and I still owe a ton on school loans. I'm totally stuck!"

Kat's expression remained the same.

"Why are you smiling at me? I just told you all this crappy news. Can't you tell that I'm frustrated and upset?"

"I know," she soothed him. "I'm so sorry you're going through all this...but maybe the timing isn't as bad as it seems."

"What?!"

Kat sat up with Noah and shared a conversation she'd had with a lawyer named Nicolas—Niko for short—who had consulted with her on her Vision. He was no longer practicing law, instead helping nonprofits create their Visions. He planned to introduce Kat to several other people who had similar Visions but were offering self-confidence in ways other than the sport of climbing. Kat recognized similarities between Noah and Niko: strong, confident, athletic, and smart.

She continued, "I asked Niko if he liked what he was doing, and he answered, 'I love it.' He realized that he hated working for other people and wanted to do some good in the world, rather than just working for money..."

Noah knew exactly where she was going with this and stopped her right there. "I'm not going to work for some nonprofit, barely eking out a living."

Kat didn't flinch. "Who said anything about 'barely eking out a living?' Niko earns high seven figures helping other people follow their dreams."

This information threw Noah for a slight loop, but he remained stubborn. "Good for Niko."

"Look, honey, hear me out," she said. "He said he desperately needs some help to accomplish his goals. I told him about you, and he was intrigued. He asked if you would be willing to chat with him."

"I don't know if I'm really the type to help others build their Visions—I'm an attorney," Noah discounted.

"So, let me get this straight," she reflected. "Your company is laying people off, they don't appreciate your talents, and you hate what you're doing—but you won't speak to someone who wants to talk to you about a new opportunity?"

Noah turned red as he realized that, by having turning things around, she'd exposed his behavior as uncharacteristically childish. "Maybe you should be the attorney."

She chuckled, pleased that she'd pierced his thick skull. "Think about it this way.

Years ago, if I'd known you were going to hit on me on the hike instead of supporting my dream to fund Cancer Boy's surgery, I probably wouldn't have agreed to have you join me. But you were authentic about wanting to help. All I ever hear you do is talk to people about their dreams and try to offer them advice on how to achieve them. Why not do it for yourself and turn it into a full-time career?"

Something lit up inside him—a tinge of excitement. "Do you really think I could do it?"

"Of course! I've always believed you could," she said, changing her tone of voice. "But I have a confession to make."

"Oh?"

"The old man and I spoke about you. He was deeply worried."

Noah slammed his fist against the mattress. "What?! Are you kidding? You kept that from me this whole time? And why didn't he talk to me personally?"

"I'm sorry, Noah—we made an agreement that I couldn't say anything until the time was right," she admitted.

"So, the time is right now? All of a sudden?"

"The old man told me that hard times give us opportunity if we remain positive. Opportunity has arrived for you, but your Mr. Negative·must be fired before you can take advantage of it."

Noah let this seep in, wondering if the old man had a point. He hadn't steered him wrong in the past.

"Do you remember what he said as he said goodbye to us?" she asked. "'La oportunidad es divertida. ¿Es divertido oportunidad?'"

Noah recalled him having made the statement but had dismissed it as rambling. He mumbled the translation aloud, as it held new significance for him: "'Opportunity is fun. Is fun opportunity?'"

Kate embraced him and declared, "Now you've got it, honey! Hey, let's go for a hike today and brainstorm. Since you're heading up an entirely new mountain, we better start doing some Vision Making!"

Chapter Ten

Instilling Energy and Fun

I knew a CEO named Lloyd who went through the Vision Maker process with great success and then recruited an army of ambassadors to spread the message. Everything seemed to be humming along fine—until the CEO conducted his annual "State of the Union" address to the entire organization. He stood up and spoke for forty-five continuous minutes about the importance of the Vision and how proud he was of the result. He thanked everyone who participated in the initiative, itemizing everyone's individual contribution in granular detail. A few minutes after having left the podium to a round of applause, Lloyd caught up with Chantelle, his Chief Marketing Officer. "Hey, Chantelle," he beamed. "How are things going?"

"Oh, everything's cool, just fine," she replied.

Even Lloyd—who wasn't the most intuitive guy in the world—could tell something was off. "Everything okay, Chantelle? You seem down about something."

"Nah, it's nothing, never mind."

"Come on, now I *know* something is wrong," Lloyd said with deep concern, leading her to a private corner of the room. "What is it? Did I say something wrong in my presentation? Did I forget to thank someone?"

"Ha!" she laughed. "You thanked *too many* people. You forgot to acknowledge your kids' hamsters."

Lloyd laughed along. "Yeah, I suppose I went a bit overboard. But I didn't want anyone to be offended being left out."

"Rest assured—you didn't leave anyone out."

"What is it, then?"

"Well, I don't know how to say this…and I hope you don't take this the wrong way…but your presentation wasn't exactly Steve Jobs."

"What do you mean?"

"I mean, people were *bored to tears*," she released.

Lloyd was incredulous. He thought it had been one of his finest speeches, filled with energy and enthusiasm. "I don't get it. I spoke about the Vision with so much passion."

"That's true," Chantelle stated. "But you must have repeated the Vision verbatim ten times. And then you explained it over and over. It's like you're saying people are too stupid to understand it… you inadvertently sounded condescending. Remember, we all helped make the Vision instantly understandable, and it resonated with people. Then you kept on going, acknowledging so many people and every little thing everybody did. It was like watching paint dry."

Poor Lloyd! Let's not be too harsh on him. He'd sunk his heart and soul into his presentation and couldn't have been more authentic. And yet, he lost his audience anyway. How might Lloyd have handled things differently?

Why So Serious?

Lloyd may have lacked the charisma of Steve Jobs, but that's not why his presentation went so far south; otherwise, his passion and sincerity would have won everyone over. Instead, he made several fatal errors stemming from innocent (and common) blind spots:

1. *Overlength:* He simply babbled on too long. Less is more!
2. *Top-down approach:* Lloyd was so excited about the Vision and what he had to share that he had tunnel vision (as it were) and became a talking head to his workforce. Thanking everyone backfired on him, as he ended up

seeming as if he was delivering an acceptance speech at the Academy Awards—except music didn't come on to cue that his time was up.

3. *Failure to involve others:* If the Vision Maker process had been so collaborative, why did Lloyd deliver the entire presentation by himself?

4. *Too serious:* Vision implementation doesn't have to be serious to be effective; nor does the language we choose. The Vision needs to be fun *and* inspiring!

The first three issues have simple solutions the next time around. Lloyd can cut down his speech to a maximum length of fifteen minutes. He might hand out an attractive document listing the Vision Maker team and their individual accomplishments. Alternatively, he could award each Vision Maker with a certificate (or other award) outside the company-wide meeting and email the list to the organization as a special "thank you" announcement. To avoid making it seem as if he's hogging the spotlight, Lloyd might delegate some stage time to members of the Vision Maker team to share their perspectives, anecdotes, and stories. Sometimes just breaking up a presentation with other faces and voices is enough to keep the attendees engaged. This also helps the event seem more down to earth and relatable to people, so it doesn't seem like "the king's speech."

Unfortunately, even if Lloyd were to correct the first three issues with his presentation, he still might not be able to overcome the fourth: *How does he make it exciting?*

Setting the Tone

The following quotes from two innovative giants explain a great deal about why these leaders were able to maintain such successful Visions:

When work becomes play, the lines between the two are flat out gone.
—Steve Jobs
There is no real difference between work and play—it's all living.
—Richard Branson

Obviously, Jobs and Branson were saying the same thing in their own way: Work needs to be like play, which means *fun*. Since Vision provides the roadmap to your future, it must be represented in the most joyous style possible at every stage. I have found that changing our mood, our aura, and even our attitude is a matter of choice. What is the story you are telling yourself about the situation you find yourself in—and how can you choose to tell a different story? What was the story that Lloyd told—that he needed to thank people for being motivated and helpful? The "fun" story could have been that his team chose to be helpful and motivated; now everyone can look at the amazing results these leaders accomplished. He might have revealed outcomes the team didn't stop to realize.

One of the most difficult challenges a leader must face is figuring out how to translate her or his passion for the Vision to a group of people who were not part of the Vision Maker team and those who seem disinterested and would much rather just go about doing their jobs. Some people who were involved in the Vision Maker process may feel they already know everything and regard sitting through a forty-five-minute speech about it is a waste of their time.

If you are in this position as a leader, sometimes the best thing to do is forego making an entire presentation of the Vision during your equivalent of a "State of the Union." You can tease about the Vision or provide a simple reminder and/or update but lace your presentation with details of extraordinary things the team accomplished. Remember: The Vision you created is bigger than you and your customer. Imagine sharing some video footage or photographs of the lives that have been impacted. It may feel like something of a letdown for you to not share your personal perspective, but the temporary disappointment will work in your favor in the long run.

If you feel you must do a complete presentation to the organization, resist the temptation to speak for more than fifteen minutes; in fact, five minutes might suffice. Then turn the stage over to the team to provide their brief insights and reflections. Before it's over, return to the Vision and enlist more people to become part of it. The power of a great Vision is that, when others see it becoming a reality, they too want to join in. Invite spouses, friends, and others who are in attendance to join the Vision if it is appropriate. Ask them to write to you with suggestions for expanding of the Vision and make their outreach easy and fun.

You can even consider organizing a periodic mastermind group or open office hours to discuss ideas from other people in attendance. Who can do all that? You!

Zapping the Vision Killers

No matter how hard you try, there will always be a Vision Killer lurking in the audience of any event, especially when it's a company presentation involving Vision. Your first inclination might be to silence the person, address the negativity in your presentation, or even snuff it out. I believe this is the wrong approach, as you'll merely antagonize the person and possibly plant the idea in other people's heads that you are concerned about being on the right track or intolerant of individual thought. Always remember: There is plenty of room for fresh opinions in your company. Invite them to suspend their issues of how to accomplish the Vision—at least for a reasonable period—and play with you on its expansion.

Imagine a heckler in a town hall meeting who wishes to speak her or his mind. Let him or her speak, even if the tone sounds confrontational and the point is off base. When you have a moment to intercede, acknowledge the person's perspective, but bring everything back to the Vision—not the criticism of execution. You might say, "You bring up a valid point on execution, but imagine with us for a bit. What's wrong with feeding the world? If you could suspend your execution questions for a little while, you may be proven right later—but imagine if your perspective changes from building the Vision." Consider invoking a discussion about how the Vision itself would create a solution to the execution issue. "What if we could find a person to solve that issue who would be willing to support this Vision?" As you answer the question, don't feel the need to agree with the heckler. Take a deep breath and move to the other

end of the stage and address the audience as a whole; this demon-
strates that you are thinking in terms of the wider community, not
just one person. If the heckler is insulting, laugh it off and move on.
People will see her or him as the villain, not you.

Every speaker involved in presenting a Vision must position
things to allow an atmosphere that welcomes safe curiosity. Audience
members need to be heard and their concerns acknowledged. Since
the Vision has now been established, organizational leaders shouldn't
table old points raised about execution. However, if it's a new execution challenge, consider inviting the team to revisit the Vision with
the execution issue in mind. Can adding more time to the Vision
potentially solve the issue?

Certain employees might pose challenges in a way that comes
across as aggressive and threatening to the Vision, but no responder
should take the bait. Return with a smile and invite them to join the
fun of Visioning while seeking solutions to the challenges. This often
creates a more collaborative discussion, instead of a defensive under-
current trying to establish who is right. Giving grace to those who
draw lines in the sand can reveal great insight into potential solutions.

For starters, there may not be any intent to disrupt things; it
could be a genuine issue that troubles this worker more than others
for whatever reason. Secondarily, the Vision Maker team has been
putting these off long enough, and it's now time to address them.

This doesn't necessarily mean that you or any of the other Vision
Makers will have immediate solutions to the execution problems.
Objectors in the audience may press hard for them, but there is no
need to "wing it" if the answers don't exist. One way to handle this is
to flip the script and say, "That is a great point, Haider. We need to
spend some time figuring that out. How would you like to organize
and lead the team to propose solutions?"

Haider is put on the spot and must take ownership of the issue or
else risk being looked upon as someone insincere who is just looking
to incite doubt.

Fun Time!

For a Vision to receive all the immediate attention and love it deserves, the leader needs to spend much less time talking and more on figuring out how to engage people. Earlier, I used the word *fun*—a word that is subject to interpretation from one person to the next. What one person enjoys doing—such as game playing and competition—another will loathe. Some people relish a break from the daily grind with an activity, whereas others are thinking about what a waste of time it is when there is "real work" to get done. The easy answer—which I'll repeat again—is that the leader must underscore the point that Vision *is* genuine work; in fact, it's the most important thing that needs to be done in the organization. It's a privilege to be involved in the spreading of the Vision's message. At the end of the day, though, accept that you'll never be able to please (or entertain) everyone; there will always be a few sticks in the mud, and that's okay. They'll just have to grin and bear it. You'll no doubt win them over as the activities kick into gear.

The "Earn a Commission on Vision" Game

This competition is easy to explain and initiate. Everyone gathers into preassigned teams of four (or six for an extra-large group). Usually, this works best if the people matched together are from different departments and don't normally interact with each other.

Team members pair up, with one person as a sales rep and the other as a client (buyer). The rep has sixty seconds to pitch a company product or service to the buyer *utilizing the essence of the Vision Statement.* Then they switch roles. When they are done, they mutually decide (based on who does each role best) which one will serve as rep and which one as client to make the pitch to their team. All pairs pitch to the team. When this round is done, the team chooses the best rep/client pair to present to all teams.

Each team has five minutes to help their rep/client champion partners give the best pitch exchange to each other incorporating the Vision. The real competition begins with each rep/client duo giving their pitch in front of everyone. The leaders of the organization cast votes to determine first, second, and third place. Cash or thoughtful prizes could be awarded to the three winning pairs and the entire team that finished first.

This game yields at least five invaluable benefits:

1. Cross-departmental interaction and teambuilding.
2. Active engagement with the Vision to instill its message in everyone's psyche.
3. Real-world application of the Vision, associating it directly with the company's product or service.
4. Identification of new applications of the Vision.
5. Fine-tuning the message to people outside the organization.

The Vision Match Game

In this game, two contestants are randomly pulled out of a hat to compete one-on-one against each other. On one whiteboard is a list of six-to-eight well-known companies. On another whiteboard are six-to-eight Vision statements. The winner of a coin toss gets to try to make a match between any company name and a corresponding Vision. She or he gets a point for a correct answer and a point deduction for one that is incorrect. The opposing player follows and does the same thing. This continues until all companies and Visions are matched. The player with the most points is the winner. The winner can continue to play another round until she loses, or two new contestants may be brought up. It could be played as a "last person standing" type of game or simply as individual matchups.

Gamers' Delight

Let's face it: The younger generations love games they can play right on their devices. In fact, many schools already employ them to make learning fun and engaging. Kahoot!, one of the most popular accepted educational gaming platforms—https://kahoot.com/—provides leaders with the opportunity to customize games and questions, so everyone in attendance can play at the same time. The objective is to not only choose the correct answer, but to input it faster than the competition. The system keeps a timer and ongoing scoring list. When the list of questions is done, you can award a prize to the winner with the most overall points.

The Impact Story Game

We often create a Vision knowing its impact will be real, but we don't yet have a relatable story to share to help people visualize it clearly. Manifesting the Vision into a scenario can help bridge that gap. I refer to this as the "The Impact Story Game."

The group is divided into teams, each of which is tasked with creating a story depicting the Vision's impact on the lives of people. The team can create—or even act out—any scenario; the more creative, the better. To inspire you, I provided the story below, which is based on an actual Vision from a real company.

> *Shirley was a single mom, by no choice of her own. Tex, the father of her child, abandoned the family after he was asked to stop drinking alcohol. He drank in such excess every day that he couldn't hold a job or be a good husband and father. Tex's troubles forced Shirley to become the breadwinner in the household, preventing her from continuing her educational path toward earning an MBA.*
>
> *Shirley was always interested in helping companies with their marketing, and she had talent to spare in this area. All her friends and acquaintances would ask for her advice on their marketing initiatives. Encouraged by her community, she started her own marketing firm. She worked hard but could only do it in her spare time, as she needed the income from her steady job to pay the bills. She also had some gaps in her knowledge—especially because she "hated numbers"—that held her back.*
>
> *One day, Shirley saw a simple ad from a financial expert named Steven Carnegie, with a fractional CFO company: "Know your numbers and you will create profitability." The ad offered a free download and even a no-commitment tu-*

torial on his services. She took advantage of both and was impressed with the results, especially since Steven offered to handle her books on a contingency consultant basis with the following promise: "If I cannot make you profitable enough and increase your net income, you do not need to pay me."

Shirley had nothing to lose and employed Steven Carnegie to provide CFO services, merging his business concept into her own. Steven taught her how to manage her expenses and income ratios and provided her with a wealth of financial advice.

Thanks to Steven's guidance, it only took a few months for Shirley's revenue and profits to soar. She was able to quit her other job and work full-time as head of her company and pay Steven, while continuing to balance work with being a single mom. One year later, she was named Entrepreneur of the Year in her town.

Steven couldn't have been prouder. What impressed him the most was Shirley's willingness to tell stories about her numerous clients who were impacted by the excellent services they provided.

Both Steven and Shirley are now famously generous with their time, sharing their advice and wisdom with anyone who needs it. Steven's company Vision was straightforward: "We want to empower others in our community to become profitable entrepreneurs, and their businesses will in turn educate and provide guidance to others in the community, uplifting the entire economy in our inner city. We just happen to carry out this Vision through CFO services."

What a great story! The Vision is huge, far bigger than Shirley and Steven individually. They embraced the Vision and shared stories of their mutual successes. Shirley was rewarded with accolades for her meaningful contributions.

Can you picture a Shirley in your community? Does your company provide anything comparable to hers? To sustain momentum with the

Vision internally and externally, tell your story of your successes with clients. Keeping them to yourself doesn't have a single benefit, except to limit the expansion of your message and the business itself.

In this chapter, I provided four activities that you can use to engage your teams with the Vision. Don't feel limited to them! You can tweak and adapt them to serve your needs and style—or create entirely new ones. Better yet, ask your teams for exciting things you can do to memorialize the Vision in the hearts and souls of your organization and beyond.

Well, we've had enough fun and games for now. It's time to chart your next evolution for growth.

Chapter Eleven

Charting the Next Evolution of Growth

Most of our journey has been about creating *your* company Vision, *your* ethos, and, of course, *your* efforts to benefit *your* company. There is great satisfaction in building on a practical strategy, taking what exists and improving it, and deriving pleasure as you watch it come together and soar. Yet, despite all your excellent Vision Making, strategic planning, and goal execution, do you ever feel as if you somehow missed driving your business those three revolutionary steps forward that would have put you over the top? What could you possibly have overlooked or done differently?

Where Are We? A 10,000-Foot View of Vision

A few decades ago, the Yellow Pages and the White Pages—those thick-as-a-brick books that listed addresses and phone numbers of businesses and residents—owned the search directory marketplace. In fact, they had something of a monopoly in this arena and were leaders in the world of print business advertising.

Then the Internet exploded on the scene. Google adopted and revolutionized the Yellow Pages model and added a powerhouse search engine that enabled browsers to find anything they wanted with just a few quick keystrokes. What did the Yellow Pages do to compete against Google? Nothing. What did the dominating, highly profitable telecom businesses—such as Pacific Bell, Verizon, and AT&T—do to counter Google? The same thing—nothing. They kept collecting old revenue without adding any Visionary strategy or special offers to their prized long-term customers.

Imagine what would have happened if these giants had applied their considerable talent and market reach to creating a strategy that would have awarded their best customers with prime first placement in the transition over to the Internet. The Yellow Pages, the White Pages, and the telecom giants never made any such effort, and eventually, the print editions of the directories became irrelevant, while Verizon, AT&T, and the like missed out on billions of dollars in revenue that went to Google.

There are countless examples of this in virtually every industry. Blockbuster Video was ousted from the video rental business because they didn't attempt to compete with Netflix, first in terms of late fee policies and second when it came to flipping over to streaming services. The Borders Group shuttered its bookstores due to overexpansion, lack of product diversification, and, worst of all, the failure to compete with Amazon.com (and even BarnesandNoble.com) for online retail sales. In the photographic industry, Kodak—a behemoth in sales of camera film—became a dinosaur as cameras and phones gained the capacity to take digital pictures.

This is the nightmare worst case scenario of every business enterprise. How do you foretell the future and know if the next disruptive innovation will be the one that will leave your business in the dust? What if investing in the next big thing and transforming your business too soon without proof could equally lead to bankruptcy? This is where taking a 10,000-foot view of Vision becomes your greatest ally in securing the boldest future possible.

From Practical to What If...

The practical lesson to be gleaned from the Yellow Pages/telecom industry downfall is obvious. Early on, they should have done something radical to assimilate the Internet into their existing business models. Specifically, the telecom companies needed to develop a brand-new service for their Yellow Pages customers. They certainly had the capability and preexisting knowledge that would have given them a significant head start over Google.

There is another evolutionary opportunity that can provide insight and even greater impact. Imagine the colossal leap telecom leaders could have taken if they had devoted capital and resources toward helping businesses find, reach, and target customers, which Google adopted fifteen years later. There was also potential for the reverse—customers discovering products and services ahead of the competition through a specific search. Eventually, that is what Google did with local business search, and look at the result today: a financial juggernaut valued in the trillions. They created something truly unique and beneficial. We must do the same in our industries or else face the risk of someday becoming obsolete.

As you evolve your company Vision, it must focus on the creation of new ideas not yet in use—perhaps not even imagined by anyone as a realistic possibility. You must shift beyond the status quo and ask *What if?* questions, such as:

> *What if…your business was to convert from B2B to B2C or vice-versa?*
>
> *What if…your product became so small it could be held in one hand?*
>
> *What if…your business was to expand and go global?*
>
> *What if…you were to create a less expensive product for lower income people—or the reverse, a high-end product for wealthy people?*
>
> *What if…your product was to go completely green?*
>
> *What if…your product or service was to become customizable?*
>
> *What if…you could solve the most unsolvable issue pertaining to your industry?*
>
> *What if…you could identify and solve an unmet customer pain point?*

What if...your business model was to become completely automated?

What if...an unbelievable advancement depicted in a science fiction story, TV show, or film could be made possible?

What if...you might be able to blend two unrelated business concepts into one?

As a current example, let's look at AI (artificial intelligence), one of the biggest technologies taking the world by storm and causing massive disruption. Putting aside the myriad controversies—for example, proprietary artistic rights, content attribution and copyright ownership, threats to occupations that could become obsolete, and deep fakes—there are clear upsides for entrepreneurs to mine, if they act with a sense of urgency. Dramatic moves into the AI arena are an imperative, as the technology will soon be able to perform most rote functions faster—and, in some cases, better when creativity isn't involved—than human beings. Technology can identify stock trends, determine business pricing models, research competition, predict consumer behavior, assist with medical diagnoses, handle physical labor that might be dangerous to people, and much more. What AI cannot do is create beyond that which exists—and that is what business entrepreneurs—such as you and me—must do.

The upshot: *We need to evolve and become more adept at creating what does not exist utilizing AI or suffer the same extinction as the Yellow Pages.*

A New Model Beyond Practicality

There are many times when practicality is essential to our efforts, such as when we are marketing and selling a new product line and must bring in revenue. However, we should never favor practicality at the expense of evolving beyond what we see before us. Consider Kat and Noah. They didn't have any conception of Noah changing the trajectory of his career until circumstances thrust him into broadening his mindset. Prior to his demotion, he could only see what was right in front of him. He wasn't thinking like a Visionary with limitless possibilities. Imagine if years earlier he had asked himself the simple question, "What can I do with my ability to support others that hasn't been done before?" He would have lit up with excitement and *acted* instead of only seeing the limits of his current situation.

This is the new model of Vision. No longer will people find their true calling from their day jobs or from books that identify career directions to explore. It will arise from the imaginations of individuals who peer into the future, ask *What if...?* questions, and take a bold leap while the window is still open.

I don't pretend to provide all the answers on the new model; I am merely initiating the conversation on the subject. My objective is to inspire you to play with your Vision and assess how it might be utilized to maintain relevance in the eye of the storm: *constant disruption.* I am urging you to commit to a life of Vision, generating revolutionary ideas from a think tank-like environment. When you nurture a Vision that is bigger than you and produce products or services that don't exist at the present time, you build the capability to own your entire market segment.

Several CEOs I know provided me with the following brilliant ideas that tap into this new model:

- How might an attorney use AI to discover the most effective legal arguments?
- How might a gifting company use AI to anticipate their customers' needs and wants based on their Facebook posts?
- How might painting contractors use AI to improve their ability to train others?
- How might an event planner use AI to create a personal experience for hundreds of conference attendees?

Take a few moments and write down a few major shifts that are happening—or about to occur—in the business world at large or in your specific industry. Identify how each one can potentially harm your business if you do nothing. Next, close your eyes and think about what your business would look like if it were to successfully lead the pack of companies that *embrace* the disruption and lead the trend. You know the drill by now: Don't Vision Kill. Open your eyes and write down all the outcomes you envisioned. Read over what you wrote and identify which scenario you think is the most appealing. Does it fit into a Vision that is bigger than you?

Always Follow Your Vision—Not Practicality

As we head toward the end of our journey, it's fun to look further on the horizon at what is in store after the Vision has been created, memorialized, and evangelized internally and externally. Some organizations perform extremely well through the first year but then lose momentum as the daily grind gets in the way and everyone reverts to spending more time putting out fires than envisioning the future and executing the steps needed to get to the promised land.

I get it. Bad things happen. Distractions run rampant: the economy takes a downturn, technology disrupts your industry, well-funded competitors steal your thunder, people leave your company, equipment breaks down, important clients or buyers shut down, and so on. When these events occur, however, it becomes *even more crucial* to focus on the Vision, so the organization can find the right direction and inspiration by rediscovering its roots.

Momentum on the Vision can also get equally as lost when a company hits a lucky streak and then just coasts along. Is the organization still making all the necessary moves that will bring the Vision closer to becoming a reality?

If your business wants to experience the next evolutionary phase of growth, the key is to prepare for the barriers before they occur and use your Vision as the tether.

Closing the Gaps

Some people love *closure*: As soon as one task is completed, they move straight on to the next. Others detest closure, feeling as if a project can always stand greater improvement and refinement. According to the Myers-Briggs Type Indicator (MBTI)—a tool used to determine the personality type of an individual—people fall into one of two camps:

- *J* for *Judging*: Those who enjoy structure, list-making, and completing tasks one at a time. Judging refers to quick decision-making and closure, not being "judgmental" about things.

- *P* for *Perceiving*: Those who prefer flexibility in their lives and how their time is managed. Sometimes they miss deadlines because they get excited by new ideas—even if they material-ize at the last minute—and want to work on something until they feel it's 100% right (which typically never happens).

Generally, there isn't a right or wrong when it comes to Judging versus Perceiving. Both have pros and cons, depending on the situation, the person's role, and to what extent one plants their flag on either end of the spectrum. In the case of Vision, the Judging work personality will do an excellent job planning, scheduling, and finaliz-ing the Vision but might struggle with any last-minute suggestions/changes to it, as well as having to continuously keep it on the docket as something fresh, alive, and in the minds and hearts of all stakehold-ers. The individual with strength in Perceiving may beat the Vision to death and change it so much and so often that it might drive everyone nuts (especially those who tilt to the Judging side).

As with most things, balance is required. The leader needs to be able to accept a final iteration of the Vision that is broadcast to the world. At the same time, she or he must be able to continue to encour-age the ongoing mission of finding creative ways to expand and share the Vision and be open to finessing it when genuine growth oppor-tunities arise that make it even bigger than first imagined. When the right balance occurs—which might require the counsel of trusted advisors in one direction or the other—the company is poised for growth into the stratosphere, all thanks to the Vision.

When to Take a Leap

There is always the conundrum that occurs when something new and exciting—but accompanied by inherent risk—comes along. The leader with unbridled entrepreneurial spirit is always gung-ho and ready to flip the switch and chase after the latest shiny object. In this scenario, there is a chance of major loss but also the possibility of a big payoff. One too many unfortunate longshot bets could send a company into bankruptcy.

Meanwhile, the ultra-conservative leader says *No* to everything until all the data is in, everything is aligned, and the risk is minimal. The problem here, of course, is that the organization passes on potentially lucrative deals (opportunity cost) and remains flat. A company in which every idea is vetoed generally has low morale among the ranks, with few people willing to stick their necks out to propose and/or support something unique and innovative.

Making the right decision in these circumstances can make or break an organization in terms of hindering or accelerating growth while ensuring that proper guardrails are in place. This is precisely when "the test" comes in. By this I mean abiding by the following statement:

If the opportunity fits in with the company Vision and leads to growth and profit, it's well worth taking the risk, assuming there are no obvious flashing red warning lights.

When a leader approaches me with uncertainty about a major investment, I always pose two questions: "*How* does it fit your Vision?" and "Can we test it?" If it doesn't harmonize with and propel the Vision, drop it immediately—no matter how lucrative it might seem. It might lead to inventing the next iteration of the smartphone, but that doesn't mean it's the right move for your organization. If anything, it's a distraction from going after your main initiatives that drive the Vision forward.

By the same token, if the opportunity fits the Vision statement, don't hesitate another moment—take that leap! Once you make the decision to *Go*, fully commit to testing it and, if you see its profitability potential, double-down on efforts to ensure success. Any time some-one questions the decision, demonstrate how it aligns with the Vision. If you connect the dots for people, they will track with you every step of the way.

Don't Go It Alone

As I've mentioned several times, a business Vision isn't—and never should be—the exclusive property of the company's leader. It was cre-ated for everyone with the primary intent of being shared widely and savored. If the leader hoards the Vision, its messaging gets clouded and suppressed in her or his mind. I've seen the same scenario play out from one company to the next as time passes post-Vision creation: The leader intentionally or unintentionally creates the impression of Vision ownership, so other people back away from it.

Zapping the Vision Killers

A Vision Killer manipulation that can surface at any time is when someone scoffs at the statement or process by saying, "Oh, the Vision? That's just for the people on the top floor—especially Lois in the corner office with the view."

Don't let anyone hide behind a hierarchy that doesn't exist. (Or, if it does to any extent, ditch it right away!) When you hear com-ments along these lines, deflate them with the following response: "That's not true. The Vision is for *everyone*, including you and me. If you're feeling left out, let's talk about ways we can bring you in."

The disparity between the leader—perhaps all members of the management team—and the rest of the workforce is often inno-cent. Leadership is talking from an altitude of 10,000 feet, so the people on the ground doing the work—especially new employees—can overcome struggles and connect with it. While attempting to be aspirational and inspirational, their words are wafting in the air and end up not being registered or adopted by the rest of the workforce.

A leader needs to be deliberate with the Vision, working with the team to make it understandable and relatable to all stakeholders at every turn. The leader can't assume that people remember it from last time or were even present that day. This is where the learnings from the fun and games in the last chapter can come in handy. The examples used during those exercises might be restated by the department heads. If the events or takeaways have faded over time, it may be time to create new engaging games—particularly to involve recently onboarded individuals. During these activities, the goal is for every employee to come up with examples of duties that connect with the Vision and the big picture. This can even become part of standing team meetings with the department head asking the question, "Does anyone have a Vision story or connection to share?"

If you ever find yourself alone in your continuing Vision quest, take the initiative and engage the troops right away!

Alignment of the Vision

Sometimes the Vision trail gets lost or distorted in the broadening, translation, or execution process. While you don't want to micromanage your direct reports or teams, you also need to know the degree to which the Vision is taking hold. Even the slightest whiff that something is off may be an indicator that some people have veered off the path.

When you meet with your direct reports and/or team, ask the following questions:

1. What are your major initiatives or projects—as well as those of your team members—and how do they tie in with the Vision?
2. If there are any tasks that do not relate to the Vision, what would happen if you were to end them today?
3. Are there unavoidable tasks unrelated to the Vision that have firm deadline/closing dates that may be accelerated?

4. What new projects have been launched that tie in with the Vision? How are they progressing?
5. Are there any stumbling blocks in executing the Vision-related projects? If so, is there anything I can do to help remove them and/or support you?
6. How are our customers, partners, and vendors reacting to the Vision?

The challenge is that you can never assume the Vision has been fully processed in the minds and hearts of your workforce. While people might nod their heads and say they support it, they may not have fully figured out the importance of assimilating it into their day-to-day efforts—or just don't know how to go about doing it. This is where simply asking the above questions can be revealing and instructive.

The Millennial Mystique

In Chapter One, I asserted that what Millennials have added to the conversation can be evolutionary in connecting Vision to company growth. Millennials, who comprise nearly 75% of the workforce, thrive on purpose. They are searching for ways to merge their personal need to contribute to the larger community with their workplace activity. It has been estimated that 63% of Millennials want to "improve society" more than "generate profit." According to the Society for Human Resource Management (SHRM), 94% of Millennials want to work toward helping a cause.

Whether your organization is profit or nonprofit, you have a prime opportunity to direct your Vision toward recruiting motivated people from this sizeable generation and then tapping into their massive potential to do good. This will not only help further the "bigger than you" aspiration of your Vision, but it will also please investors/shareholders, Board members, as well as external partners, buyers, vendors, and even customers who prefer to do business with organizations that are authentic in their efforts to improve society. Other generations working in your organization will see and feel the results—which includes brand loyalty, in addition to growth, so they will eventually come around and add even more numbers and power to the effort.

You may be seeing it happen already: The companies that combine Vision with a commitment to making a difference in society—including Tom's, Burt's Bees, Wegmans, Google, and Tesla, to name a few—are among the most successful. Those that fail to accomplish this will, unfortunately, go the way of huge businesses that didn't see the writing on the wall or peer into the future, such as the earlier referenced print Yellow Pages, Blockbuster, and Kodak.

Are you ready to change the world? Turn the page to Chapter Twelve and you'll find out how—from within.

Chapter Twelve

Changing the World

Several years ago, I was relaxing and enjoying a beer at Froggies—a quaint bar in Anaheim, California—when I happened to meet a graduate student named Naveen, who was working on his PhD in chemistry. Froggies wasn't exactly a hub of academia—the only other customers were some guys watching a rugby contest on TV and a few others who were huddled around a pool table—so I thought it curious when a studious-looking young man happened to appear next to me at the bar counter. He seemed so down and out that I felt compelled to turn to him and blurt, "I hope you don't mind my asking—are you okay? You seem to be terribly upset about something."

"Oh no," he chuckled. "It's not what you think. It's not like I had a death in the family or was dumped by my girlfriend or anything like that. I'm just struggling to figure out a scientific project I'm working on for my PhD."

His response intensified my curiosity. I ordered another round of beers for the two of us, and we made proper introductions. After some small talk, I said, "Naveen, I don't know a thing about chemistry. I couldn't tell you if your presumptions make sense or if you are running your experiments correctly. But, if you share with me what you are doing and what is going wrong, perhaps I can serve as some kind of sounding board for you."

He slurped back some beer and grinned. "Sure, why not, I'm game," he said. "I've spent the last three years going around in circles with this, I've talked to my academic advisers and every person at school, so it couldn't hurt to tell it to someone on the outside."

He went on to describe how he was working on proving a theory that required an intermediary chemical reaction to achieve a final chemical compound. Unfortunately, the result was instantaneous and, therefore, too difficult to document. "I don't know what to do," he ruminated. "My entire life and career are on the line. It's not just about earning my PhD. If my ideas are on track, they will be implemented into a patent and later monetized. I can't afford to fail, but I just don't see any kind of path to a solution. I'm feeling lost…"

He expressed his frustration for the next several minutes. I listened.

"I'm so sorry you are going through this, Naveen," I comforted him when he was finished. "Your project is indeed way over my head—but I would like to ask one general question, if that's all right."

"Sure—have at it!"

"Since you already know the final chemical compound, might you be able to prove the intermediate chemical reaction by progressing backward to create your original product?"

He explained in what seemed to me like ancient Greek why this wasn't remotely feasible. "It's just impossible…" He was acting a bit like a Vision Killer to me, but I found myself unable to articulate this sentiment to him at that moment.

A drunk local rugby fan overheard my new friend's declaration and chimed in, "If my team can win today against this team, *anything* is possible." The three of us laughed, and the rugby fan turned his attention back to shout an obscenity at the game on the TV.

Naveen and I finished up our drinks and drew our conversation to a friendly close. "Well, Naveen, I'm sorry to say, it doesn't look like we're going to solve your chemical reaction dilemma today. But don't give up hope—keep trying!"

We exchanged email addresses and phone numbers and said goodbye to each other. Frankly, I didn't think I was going to hear from

Naveen again, but one week later, I was pleasantly surprised to see his name and number pop up on my phone. "*Jim, Jim! It's me—Naveen! From Froggies!*" he exclaimed.

"Hi, Naveen, great hearing from you," I said, unable to come close to his level of enthusiasm. "You sound really excited about something. What is happening?"

"I did it, I did it! I proved the intermediary reaction!"

"Congratulations! How did you manage to pull it off?"

"Well, first…you inspired me to keep going, so thank you for that," he conveyed. "But you won't believe this—the real game changer was actually that drunk rugby fan."

I could hardly believe what I was hearing. "*Him?* Really? How?"

"The drunk fellow was onto something. He said, 'If my team can win today against this team, *anything* is possible.' That statement kept coming back into my head for some reason. The intermediate chemical reaction could not win, so I put a buffer, a ringer—like the drunk dude—into the mix, and *voila!* It worked."

You are no doubt wondering why I'm sharing this story with you at the beginning of this final chapter. My point is that each person wields the power to change the world, as well as the capability of helping others do so. Even something seemingly innocuous like a drunk making a goofy joke at a bar can have significant impact.

When we have a Vision, we must be open to collaborating with anyone and everyone. We want to cast a wide net to recruit as many cheerleaders as possible, at every level. Naturally, you want brilliant minds and experts to chime in—but you never know when a drunk rugby fan might pop up out of nowhere and provide the miracle you are looking for at just the right moment in time. Imagine what more you might be able to accomplish by tacking on things such as additional mastermind sessions, group think tanks, and social media group chats to your current efforts. The possibilities and applications become endless, particularly if you do not allow a Vision Killer to intercede!

Start Creating Your Legacy Now

I'm sure at some point in your life you have thought about what might be written in your obituary or said about you in a eulogy at your funeral (which is a long time away from now, don't worry!). I'll bet that, when you visualize them in your head, they don't read or sound like a laundry list of jobs, surviving family members, and individual accomplishments. You are looking for statements encapsulating a life that was well led and driven by purpose. And, since you've followed the program in the first eleven chapters of this book, you already know that purpose is driven by Vision.

At this stage, the questions you should be asking yourself about your Vision are whether it has the potential to create the legacy you desire, if you can imagine it existing beyond your time on earth, and whether you are setting your sights high enough to make a favorable difference upon this world and positively impact as many people as possible. It's not about financial reward, personal recognition, and achievement; those things are nice side fringe benefits and make you feel good in the now, while you are still living and breathing. What rewards you most in the end is the great joy and internal satisfaction of making a genuine difference. Sure, this phrase is said all the time, but now you have the opportunity and the understanding to make it happen. What sticks after you've left this world is what matters most and forms your true legacy.

Your Vision, therefore, isn't just about you and your business. While both are extremely important, they don't need to be the prime focus. When you direct your attention to improving the world at large and the imprint you can make on it, you and your business will flourish. Let's look at how we can turn that desire into a reality...

The Role of Your Vision in Social Consciousness

The Dalai Lama once said, "The creation of a more peaceful and happier society has to begin from the level of the individual, and from there it can expand to one's family, one's neighborhood, to one's community, and so on."

This statement drives home the notion that Vision starts with the self but must then flow outward to the rest of the world. Whether you realize it or not at this moment, your Vision has the power to impact everything under the sun: poverty, hunger, disease, world peace, pollution, and even political divisiveness. Consider for a moment how much Martin Luther King Jr., Mother Teresa, and Mahatma Gandhi contributed to society. Each did so by first having a unique personal Vision but then broadening it to involve the masses. Don't underestimate yourself and refuse to believe that you are incapable of such feats. The evolution of Vision in society isn't farther than your hand in front of you, as long as your desire to create remains as unobstructed as it has ever been.

The rest of us who have a Vision are often missing one key ingredient that Dr. King, Mother Teresa, and Gandhi developed in abundance: *collaboration*. Once their Visions were in place, they were able to brilliantly communicate them to others and engage and enroll them to further the causes. One person may be able to accomplish what seems to be a miracle, but the reality is that she or he made it happen by tapping into a much wider collective. Imagine any one of the three alone on a deserted island. The impact would have no sense of achievement, as their efforts were all about the people who joined the Vision. The Civil Rights Movement, for example, would never have transpired if Martin Luther King Jr. had kept his dream to himself.

Permit me to be even more direct. If you aren't using the unique gifts bestowed on you, you are limiting *our* destiny in this world. It is not then, it is now; and it is not *resuming*, it is *starting*. Becoming a better person means dedicating your life to serving the world as an unbridled Vision Maker.

When you share a Vision that provides social value on a grand scale, I guarantee many people will at first ignore you, turn you down flat, provide all kinds of reasons why it won't work (including "You can't do that by yourself!"), and perhaps even mock you.

To help zap these Vision Killers, you might consider sharing the story of billionaire—well, *former* billionaire, to be exact—Chuck Feeney, who is still alive as of this writing. Feeney became a billionaire decades ago as cofounder of airport retailer Duty Free Shoppers—but this wasn't nearly fulfilling enough for him. He founded The Atlantic Philanthropies in 1982 with the Vision "Investing in a Better Future for All" and accompanying tagline "Giving While Living." More than four decades later, Feeney has donated *$8 billion* to charities, an amount that is worth *375,000%* of his current net worth. He is quite content living a plentiful—although far less garish—existence, rather than having lived for so many years without doing all he could to make the world a better place. Bill Gates and Warren Buffett are among the wealthy giants who have been inspired by Feeney's Vision to follow in his footsteps.

Now *that* is what I call a legacy!

We Tend to Care Only When It Impacts Us

It's human nature for us to only care about a cataclysmic event when it specifically connects to something we see and feel in our immediate lives. For example, we all know certain politicians who declined aid to other states that were devastated by hurricanes but then demanded such assistance when it happened in their own backyards.

In June 2023, an unusual thing occurred in New York, New Jersey, Pennsylvania, and Connecticut: Massive amounts of smoke from wildfires in Quebec drifted south and overtook the skies, blanketing the air with an orange apocalyptic hue, making the air almost unbreathable. Residents of these areas witnessed several days of shock and awe; they'd never experienced anything like it before and were understandably upset. What they probably didn't consider is that California residents contend with raging wildfires *every single year,* and it was only three years earlier that five of the state's ten worst wildfires occurred, one of which burned *over a million acres of property.* The air quality was certainly a major concern, but far from the only one.

For the most part, we all believe that clean drinking water is a basic human right. It might shock you to find out that nearly 3,000 locations across fifty states in America have water that is contaminated with unsafe levels of harmful chemicals. Is it possible you have a friend, relative, or business associate who lives in one of those areas? Or that perhaps you might unknowingly end up in one of them yourself as a visitor or even a resident?

At this stage, some of you may be thinking that I'm preaching and going off on a "woke" soapbox. The fact of the matter is that it's *good business* for us all to care about one another's Visions for a better world. This isn't only a result of not knowing whether the roles will someday reverse. It's also because we start to feel genuinely purposeful—a meaningfulness that exceeds our desire for wealth and bestows on us a genuine sense of pride. Imagine an America that amplifies—or revitalizes, if you believe it's been lost—this feeling in all of us.

We've already seen the impact of climate change in the rise of previously mentioned wildfires, an increased number of fierce storms, the melting of the polar icecaps, and the diminished size of certain lakes (notably, Lake Mead). With all this evidence, many people continue to deny the reality of climate change or may be coming around to acceptance of the concept yet won't support efforts to reverse it because they don't see how the issue directly impacts them—or, worse, they feel powerless to do anything about it on an individual level.

If you're still stuck on soaring profits or just paying the bills to keep things afloat, be aware that apathy has never led to the creation of anything substantial or lasting. The sentiment "nothing will ever change" ensures that nothing ever will. You are already throwing in the towel, along with the opportunity to create a Vision that would have the potential to change the world.

A Revolutionary Vision

With continuous technological improvements and the ability to collaborate with anyone around the world in real time, it becomes advantageous for us to reinvent the model of Vision. We should never think along the lines of "it's *their* Vision, not mine," but rather, "this is *our* shared Vision." Who cares about credit and ownership when we all seek the same desirable outcome?

The Vision "revolution"—yet to be discovered but not specifically offered at this point—is to implement a central hub (a social media site, an app, a virtual reality-type entity, or something yet to be invented) in which Vision can tackle any issue facing our world today. This utopian platform would serve as a business model that equally encourages profit and nonprofit organizations and rewards individuals for collaborative, engaged participation. I imagine the enterprise would initiate with Vision as the starting point; one person would plant the seed, after which others would metaphorically fertilize it, water it, and add sun to help it sprout, grow, spread, and flourish. Think of it like crowdfunding on steroids, with the focus on building a viable, strong, and incredibly useful Vision, instead of a focus on raising money. The Vision Maker process outlined in this book would make the Vision bigger than any one person involved. Once complete, the Vision would be given a warm send-off to a think tank for implementation and execution. Toward that end, I want this book to be the start of a conversation—not just another tome on the shelf—to inspire a new Vision of what it means to create a Vision and create a discussion around the ways to amplify and enhance the program I've offered in this book. Here is my first stab at the Vision of my revolutionary Vision enterprise concept:

To make the impossible become possible through Vision.

Attention business owners, entrepreneurs, CEOs, and everyone else who has a stake in the future of our planet: This revolutionary Vision is calling out to you. Let's change the world. Together.

Afterword

The Exciting Journey Ahead

Noah met with Niko, the former attorney, who coached him on all the opportunities that could be within his grasp. Noah quit his job, and, within months, he and Kat were empowering people to fulfill their dreams in a way they never thought possible. They guided dozens of others to create what they could not see. This was the message they shared at every opportunity—especially while in the company of their amazed clients, who had continuous fun in the process.

Sources

Chapter One:
See Dorsey, Jason. *Y-Size Your Business,* John Wiley and Sons, 2010.

Chapter Five:
"In his book The Big Leap, *Gay Hendricks coined…":* Hendrick, Gay. *The Big Leap.* HarperOne, 2010.

Chapter Seven:
"As studio executive Bonnie Hammer once said…": https://www.brainy quote.com/quotes/bonnie_hammer_853294

Chapter Eight:
"Apple's Vision: To make the best products on earth and to leave the world better than we found it…": https://bstrategyhub.com/ apple-mission-statement-vision-core-values/

"…it went on to become the innovative juggernaut it is today, now valued at $2.3 trillion…": https://www.google.com/search?q=what+ is+apple+worth+today&oq=what+is+apple+worth+today&aqs= chrome..69i57j0i22i30i625l4j0i22i30j0i22i30i625j0i390l2 .3228j1j7&sourceid=chrome&ie=UTF-8

"Airbnb's Vision: Belong anywhere….": https://mission-statement .com/airbnb/#:~:text=Airbnb%20vision%20statement%20 is%20%E2%80%9CBelong,client%20can%20get%20from%20 Airbnb

"Netflix's Vision: Entertain the world…": https://about.netflix.com/en

"Looking back, the idea of 'entertaining the world'...": https://www
.macrotrends.net/stocks/charts/NFLX/netflix/net-worth#:~:
text=Interactive%20chart%20of%20historical%20
net,24%2C%202023%20is%20%24141.24B

"Similarly, Amazon—whose Vision is...": https://www.comparably
.com/companies/amazon/mission

"A physician named Dr. Raymond V. Damadian once had a Vision
that...": https://crev.info/scientists/raymond-damadian/

"Stephen King's classic novel Carrie *was rejected by thirty publishers..."*:
https://www.writingroutines.com/renowned-writers-on
-overcoming-rejection/

*"The book was indeed published, in 1974, and has reportedly
sold over..."*: https://www.seattletimes.com/entertainment/
lsquocarriersquo-by-the-numbers/

"George Bernard Shaw once said...": https://advice.theshineapp.com/
articles/29-quotes-thatll-help-calm-your-fear-of-change/

"To paraphrase 19th century UK Prime Minister Benjamin Disraeli...":
https://www.brainyquote.com/quotes/benjamin
_disraeli_154186#:~:text=Benjamin%20Disraeli%20
Quotes&text=I%20am%20prepared%20for%20the%20
worst%2C%20but%20hope%20for%20the%20best

Chapter Ten:
*"When work becomes play, the lines between the two are flat out
gone..."*: https://www.pinterest.com/pin/35677022022752717/

"There is no real difference between work and play—it's all living...":
https://www.azquotes.com/quote/825561?ref=work-and-play

Chapter Eleven:

"According to the Myers-Briggs Type Indicator…": https://www.myers
briggs.org/my-mbti-personality-type/mbti-basics/judging-or
-perceiving.htm

*"…Vision to company growth. Millennials, who comprise nearly
75% of the workforce…":* https://www.kornferry.com/insights/
this-week-in-leadership/millennials-purpose-

*"…The companies that combine Vision with a commitment to making a
difference in society…":* https://www.inc.com/rebecca-deczynski/
power-of-purpose-list-impact-driven-companies.html

Chapter Twelve:

*"The Dalai Lama once said, "The creation of a more peaceful and hap-
pier society…"* https://www.azquotes.com/quotes/topics/
contribution-to-society.html

*"…Chuck Feeney, who is still alive as of this writing. Feeney became a
billionaire decades ago…"* https://www.atlanticphilanthropies
.org/our-story

https://www.forbes.com/sites/stevenbertoni/2020/09/15/exclusive
-the-billionaire-who-wanted-to-die-brokeis-now-officially
-broke/?sh=7ed3a65f3a2a

Suggested Readings

Bernhoff, Michael. *Average Sucks*. HCI, 2020.

Cameron, Julia, and Bryan Mark. *The Artist's Way: 25th Anniversary Edition*. TarcherPerigee, 2016.

Chu, Ching-Ning. *Thick Face, Black Heart*. Balance, 1994.

Hendrick, Gay. *The Big Leap*. HarperOne, 2010.

Maltz, Maxwell. *Psycho-Cybernetics: The Search for Self-Respect*. Thought Works Books, 2022.

Maslan, Allison. *Scale or Fail*. Wiley, 2019.

Sinek, Simon. *Start with Why*. Portfolio, 2009.

Index

About the Author

Jim Ballidis

Jim Ballidis is a serial entrepreneur, attorney, inventor, investor, and venture capitalist who has owned and directed several manufacturing and service companies over the years. He has published chapters in several Amazon and *Wall Street Journal* bestselling books with such authors as Jack Canfield and David Corbin.

James was the managing partner for the California law firm of Allen, Flatt, Ballidis & Leslie, Inc., and a 1985 graduate of Southwestern Law School in Los Angeles. He was admitted to the California State Bar that same summer. Jim is associated with the Pinnacle Global Network, as a Mentor and an active member of the Board of Directors of two flourishing companies. Having mentored and discussed Vision with hundreds of CEOs and other leaders, he offers insight into the things that stop us from being our best. A reformed Vision Killer himself, he now dedicates his time to helping people and businesses create and sustain Visions that are bigger than themselves.